THE TREASURE OF THE COPPER SCROLL

JOHN MARCO ALLEGRO was born in London and served in the Royal Navy during the Second World War. He received his B.A. in Semitic languages from the University of Manchester in 1951 and his M.A. in 1952. While doing further research in Hebrew dialects at Oxford University, Mr. Allegro was called to Jerusalem as the first British representative on the international team editing the Dead Sea Scroll fragments. Since 1954 he has returned to the Dead Sea area at frequent intervals and has recorded his archaeological and philological findings in a number of articles and books, which include *The Dead Sea Scrolls* (1964), *The People of the Dead Sea Scrolls* (Doubleday, 1958), and *Search in the Desert* (Doubleday, 1964). Mr. Allegro lectures in Old Testament and Intertestamental Studies at the University of Manchester.

THE TREASURE OF THE
COPPER SCROLL

SECOND, REVISED EDITION

BY
JOHN MARCO ALLEGRO

THE OPENING AND DECIPHERMENT OF THE MOST MYSTERIOUS
OF THE DEAD SEA SCROLLS, A UNIQUE INVENTORY OF
BURIED TREASURE, WITH SOME OF THE
RESULTS OF A SURVEY CARRIED OUT
ON THE TREASURE SITES
IN THE HOLY LAND

6-0184

Anchor Books
Doubleday & Company, Inc.
Garden City, New York

The Treasure of the Copper Scroll was originally
published by Doubleday & Company, Inc. in 1960

Anchor Books edition: 1964

Grateful acknowledgment is made to the following for permission to include the copyrighted selections included in this
work:

HARVARD UNIVERSITY PRESS for excerpts from *Josephus* from
the Loeb Classical Library Edition. Reprinted by permission of
the Harvard University Press.

ABINGDON PRESS, AND HODDER AND STOUGHTON LIMITED (London) for excerpts from *The Life and Times of Herod the Great*
by Stewart Perowne. Reprinted by permission of the publishers.

*By gracious permission this book is dedicated
with the author's profound admiration and respect
to His Majesty King Hussein of Jordan*

FOREWORD

This completely revised edition of *The Treasure of the Copper Scroll*, originally published in 1960, is intended primarily for the non-specialist. The complete facsimile, transliteration, and notes of the original edition have therefore been omitted here. I have, however, continued to give bracketed references to the *Wars* and *Antiquities* of Josephus (coded JW and JA respectively) since popular translations of these important historical works find a welcome place on many non-specialists' shelves.

To keep the price of this volume as low as possible, photographs have had to be kept to a minimum, and I have taken the liberty of referring the reader occasionally to the much more complete pictorial coverage of the Scrolls story contained in my *People of the Dead Sea Scrolls* (*PDSS*).

My wife has again kindly undertaken most of the responsibility for proofreading and my thanks are also due to my secretary, Jennie Farley, for other secretarial assistance.

J.M.A.

Prestbury, Cheshire
September 1963

ILLUSTRATIONS

PLATES

Following page 66:
1. The unopened rolls of copper.
2. Henri de Contenson.
3. A roll mounted on its spindle preparatory to cutting.
4. Professor H. Wright Baker cutting a segment of the scroll.
5. A newly cut segment.
6. A segment showing part of the first column of the engraving together with a facsimile of the text.
7. Dr. Awni Dajani, Director of Antiquities, Jordan, with Professor Karl Georg Kuhn.
8. The Wadi Qumran, the ruins of the Essene monastery, and the Dead Sea.
9. Cleaning a segment of the scroll with a dental brush.
10. The completely open scroll.
11. Father Joseph T. Milik.
12. The Vale of Achor (Buqei'a) and, on the right, Hyrcania (*Khirbet [el-] Mird*).
13. Mird from the west.
14. The Herodian aqueduct at the foot of Mird.
15. Inside a Mird cistern.
16. The monument at Mird.
17. Inside the stepped tunnel at Mird.

Following page 106:
18. Examining the earthquake rift in the cistern of Khirbet Qumran.

19. Part of the silver treasure hoard discovered at Khirbet Qumran.

20. Making a sounding at the western end of the Hall of Congregation, Qumran.

21. Across the Wadi Kelt toward Taurus, seen from Cypros ("Mount Gerizim").

22. Looking from the Wadi Kelt northward toward the site of Alexandrium.

23. The outline of the Herodian fortress of Cypros from the slope of the hill.

24. Searching the cistern in Cypros.

25. The Mount of Temptation (*Docus*), looking over the tell of ancient Jericho.

26. Part of the excavations of Bethesda in the grounds of St. Anne's.

27. One of the Antonia cisterns under the Sisters of Zion Convent.

28. The chamber at the north end of the Antonia double cistern.

29. The upper Kidron Valley as it leaves Jerusalem.

30. The southeastern corner of the Haram, site of the Pinnacle of the Temple, seen from the porch of St. James's tomb across the valley.

31. The ancient Jewish tombs at the foot of the Mount of Olives: Absalom, St. James, Zechariah, and "Zadok."

32. Excavating the "Zadok" tomb.

33. Part of the lower Kidron ("Wadi of Fire") with the Mar Saba monastery.

34. The Golden Gate, Jerusalem.

LINE DRAWINGS

Figure   *page*
1. Palestine.   164
2. Scroll discoveries in the wilderness of Judaea.   165
3. Khirbet Qumran and the scroll caves.   166
4. Qumran and the Buqei'a.   167

5. Khirbet Mird (after G. R. H. Wright, *Biblica* 42 [1961]).   168

6. Plan of the Essene monastery at Qumran (after R. de Vaux, *Revue Biblique* 63 [1956], opp. p. 576).   169

7. The Wadi Kelt, Cypros, and Jericho.   170

8. Jerusalem—relief.   171

9. The Antonia fortress and the double cistern (after C. Warren and C. R. Conder, *The Survey of Western Palestine, Jerusalem*, London, 1884, opp. p. 234, and L.-H. Vincent, *Jérusalem de l'Ancien Testament*, Paris, 1956, pl. XLII).   172

10. The Shaveh and the Hinnom Valley.   173

11. (*a*) and (*b*). Wilson's Arch, the subterranean vaults, and the "secret passage" (after J. Simons, *Jerusalem in the Old Testament*, Leiden, 1952, p. 368, and C. Wilson and C. Warren, *The Recovery of Jerusalem*, London, 1871, opp. p. 81).   174

12. The Pinnacle of the Temple and the tombs in the Kidron Valley.   175

13. The southern and eastern Haram walls and rock levels (after Wilson and Warren, *The Recovery of Jerusalem*, opp. p. 119).   176

14. The Herodian Temple area (after Vincent, *Jérusalem de l'Ancien Testament*, pl. CII).   177

15. Plan and elevation of the tombs in the Kidron Valley (after N. Avigad, *Ancient Monuments in the Kidron Valley* [Hebrew], Jerusalem, 1954, opp. p. 38).   178

16. The Temple of the Mishnah (after Vincent, *Jérusalem de l'Ancien Testament*, pl. CV).   179

17. The Reservoirs of the Haram (after Warren and Conder, *The Survey of Western Palestine, Jerusalem*, opp. p. 116).   180

18. The treasure locations of the copper scroll.   181

xi

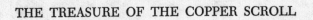

THE TREASURE OF THE COPPER SCROLL

CHAPTER ONE

The small saw screamed as it bit into the oxidized metal. A plume of fine dust followed its track. After an inch or two the operator lifted the blade and blew the surface clear. We leaned over, anxiously looking for signs of cracking, but all was well. The operator again brought the saw down and eased it into the groove. Painfully slowly it moved along the cutting line toward the edge of the scroll. Then at last the little motor whined its relief as the saw broke clear. The operator reached across to switch off the current and wiped the sweat from his brow. We smiled at each other, and relaxed. Another step had been safely taken toward unraveling one of the most exciting documents ever found.

Three years before, in the spring of 1952, some archaeologists had found a strange document lying in a cave overlooking the northwestern shores of the Dead Sea (Figures 1–3; *PDSS* Plates 71, 72). It was quite unlike anything they had ever seen before. Although at first sight it looked like a normal parchment scroll, when they brushed off the dust from its surface they found that it had been made of sheets of copper riveted together. In rolling, one line of rivets had broken apart and now it lay in two pieces against an inner wall of the cave (Plate 1).

The roof had collapsed long ago, effectively sealing its contents against the atmosphere and curious pass-

1

ers-by. Not far from the scroll the searchers found the broken remains of dozens of jars and lids, and in the debris at the back of the cave small fragments of parchment documents.

Gently the archaeologists lifted the rolls and carried them to the museum in Jerusalem. There they were cleaned and coated with a celluloid solution to prevent further deterioration. From the outside, indentations of writing could be seen punched into the inner face of the scroll, but the copper had completely oxidized, leaving a brittle substance that broke away at any attempt at unrolling. Enough could be seen to show that the writing was in Hebrew, in the large, square characters that had become increasingly familiar during recent years from other manuscript discoveries.

The cave of the copper scroll lay very near another cache of ancient documents found by an Arab shepherd five years previously (Figure 3). These were the famous Dead Sea Scrolls and their discovery had been greeted with much excitement by scholars and laymen alike. They had included copies of books of the Old Testament older by a thousand years than anything we had previously known. Furthermore, some of the scrolls were of religious works never before seen which threw a wonderful new light on the beginnings of Christianity. It seemed likely that this was only part of the library of some Jewish sect living here in the wilderness, and a search was instituted in the vicinity to find more scroll caves.

It was on 20 March 1952 that one such search party was rewarded with the discovery of the copper scroll. The group was led by a young Frenchman, Henri de Contenson, attached to the French School of Bible Studies in Jerusalem (Plate 2). This establishment, together with the American School of Oriental Research and the Palestine Archaeological Museum, had joined forces to search the cliffs for some five miles around the area of the shepherd's original discovery. They were hoping to snatch the initiative from the Arabs of the shepherd lad's tribe who, after the first fortuitous discovery, had decided to go scroll hunting in earnest. The Bedouin had learned to their chagrin that four of the original cache of seven scrolls which they had parted with for a pittance had changed hands in the United States for a quarter of a million dollars.

For a long time De Contenson's wonderful find served only to tantalize visitors to the museum. All that could be ascertained from marks visible on the surface was that it was a non-biblical text, and probably a catalogue of some kind. It had originally been composed of three sheets of metal giving a total length of eight feet and a width of eleven inches. Analysis of the crystalline substance remaining showed that the metal had been of almost pure copper and so originally quite soft and malleable. It had been beaten to a thickness equivalent to three post cards laid together.

All kinds of suggestions were offered for opening the rolls. One self-styled "prophet" wrote to the museum suggesting that they be soaked in oil and heated in an oven. They would then unroll quite easily and reveal a message written by the "prophet" himself. A professor of Old Testament in Britain suggested encasing each roll in a sheet of solid gold which would then provide a flexible backing for the brittle material when unrolled. Transmitted through the same source came an equally unprofitable idea for "photographing" the inner surface of the scroll by slipping a sheet of sensitized film between the convolutions of the rolls, packed tight though they were with dust and for all we knew, welded inseparably together.

More practical experiments were progressing in the United States on replicas of the rolls oxidized artificially to the same degree as the originals. The idea was to try progressively to replace the oxide by pure metal so that flexibility could be restored to the brittle substance. Successive reports were not overoptimistic, however, and it became clear that the most feasible means of obtaining access to the scroll's inner surface was by cutting it open.

In 1953 I was invited to join an international team of scholars called together in Jerusalem for the purposes of editing a large collection of manuscripts that had been found in the meantime in another cave in the Dead Sea area. I suggested to the Director of Antiquities of that time, an Englishman named Gerald Lankester Harding, that a suitable laboratory for undertaking this delicate operation of cutting the copper scroll might be sought in Manchester. I had recently taken up a lectureship in that English university and would thus be in a good position to sound out the possibilities and supervise the work. It was not, however, until the spring of 1955 that Harding received permission from the Jordan Government to take the matter a stage further. He asked me to find someone who would undertake the task.

I turned naturally first of all to the university's metallurgical department. The response was not overenthusiastic. The professor in charge offered to see what could be done, but when I described the approach of the American scientists in their experiments, and inquired what specific lines of research he had in mind, I was told, rather curtly, that although the professor would look at the job, he had no intention of up-

4

setting the whole routine of the department for the sake of our copper scroll.

Perhaps I had chosen a particularly unfortunate moment to pose our problem but I knew enough about the difficulties that the work would entail to realize that nothing short of a whole-hearted enthusiasm and a willingness to expend a lot of skill and patience over the operation could ensure success. I made no further approach to the university.

In Manchester there is a world-famous firm manufacturing grinding wheels, some of them fine enough to be used for splitting pen nibs. There I found much more enthusiasm but a regretful recognition that they possessed neither the machine nor the facilities for undertaking our project. That same day, a colleague of mine in the university suggested trying the Manchester College of Science and Technology, with whose principal, Dr. B. V. (now Lord) Bowden, he had been discussing my problem in the train that morning.

Bowden is a stocky man, with an unkempt mop of hair and an inexhaustible reserve of energy. He runs everyone around him off their feet and is one of the most effective scourges of complacency in high quarters about England's standing in the technological world that the Establishment has ever had to suffer. His most biting criticisms are reserved for those who believe that our educational system should cater mainly for proper tuition in the humanities and leave science and technology to the intellectually underprivileged. Yet, it was Bowden who accepted the challenge of our scroll with the greatest enthusiasm. The weeks of work that its opening would probably entail would result at best in the reading of a text that had been put away two thousand years ago. There was al-

5

most an equal chance that the operation would produce only useless scraps of oxidized metal defaced beyond recognition.

I called on Bowden the following day with photographs I had taken and explained the problem as best I could. There seemed no doubt in his mind at all that the college could undertake the work successfully. He picked up the telephone and called in the Professor of Mechanical Engineering, Dr. H. Wright Baker. Baker is an older man and more stolid than Bowden. Less excitable, yet of a rather nervous temperament, he was at first a little hesitant about accepting such an unusual commission. He described himself deprecatingly as a mere "plumber" but under the pressure of Bowden's unbounded eagerness that the college should not fail in its response to any technological problem he agreed to undertake the work.

I wrote to Harding immediately and told him of my reception at the Manchester College of Science and Technology and asked that the first of the rolls should be sent from Jordan as soon as possible. In July 1955 Harding brought the smaller of the pieces with him and delivered them personally to the college. By September when I had returned from the summer's work in Jordan, Baker had designed and built a machine for the cutting operation. It incorporated a small, one-and-three-quarter inch circular saw running on a spring-loaded arm over a pair of rails fastened to the baseboard. On these a trolley would move carrying the scroll directly under the saw. In this way the scroll itself would do the moving, the saw remaining stationary, except that the arm on which it revolved could be lowered or lifted under the fingertip control of the operator. Further embellishment included a blower by the saw blade to carry away the dust and an old magnifying glass set above it to help in keeping a strict control on the cutting.

To prevent any tendency for the brittle oxide to shatter into a thousand pieces the moment the blade touched it, the surface was to be coated with an aircraft adhesive and baked to form a pliable skin. Thus, somewhat more cheaply, the function of the solid gold sheet previously suggested would be fulfilled.

Baker showed me his machine with obvious pride, but I confess I did not find it a particularly impressive-looking instrument (Plate 4). Perhaps its rugged aspect owed something to the fact that it had been constructed almost entirely from ex-Service equipment, obtained at the end of the war through an imaginative coup on the part of the college bursar. Furthermore, when the motor was switched on the whole machine jumped convulsively on its base every time the knot on the string connecting the motor to the saw ran over its pulley wheel.

The scroll would first be skewered lengthwise by an aluminum rod with a serrated end. This would make a way through the dust packing the center of the scroll for a steel spindle which would hold the precious roll on the trolley for cutting. At each end wooden discs would be held secure against the fragile edges of the scroll with dental plaster packed between the leaves (Plate 3). Thus the whole "Swiss roll" would be held firmly for the cuts that in theory should make it possible to peel off segments one by one.

The first cutting line was clear enough: diametrically opposite the leading edge of the scroll was a margin between two columns of writing. The line we scratched on the surface for the saw to follow thus ran clear of most of the indentations visible on that side.

I left Baker on the evening of my visit to the laboratory longing to try out his machine on the first part of the scroll. It was agreed that we should make the first cut on the following morning, but I was not unduly surprised to hear his voice on the telephone that evening, telling me, between gasps for air, that he had done it. In case the worst had happened and the precious document shattered into a thousand pieces as the saw touched the surface he had wished to be alone in his misery. But all was well, and the first segment now lay open to the light ready for cleaning (Plate 5).

The following morning we made the second cut, as I have already described. This time an uneven fold in the surface of the scroll necessitated a cut only a little way on from the first and running through a column of writing. Judging where exactly to draw our line was thus more complex and the softly rounded indentations we could see were not always sufficiently distinctive to allow identification of the letters or the exact position of the engraved strokes. However, we managed to avoid cutting through most of the letters, and where this was unavoidable chose those which could be bisected without destroying their form completely.

While Baker prepared the scroll for the third cut I took up the two separated segments to clean them. The dust fell away mercifully easily. A light scraping removed most of it and then a gentle brushing revealed the bright yellowish-green surface of the inner face. It was a thrilling moment. For the first time in two thousand years the face of this strange scroll lay open to the light. All those many centuries ago some unknown person had tried to communicate a message that he deemed important enough to inscribe on sheets of copper. I laid the pieces gently on the table side by side and took up pencil and paper.

CHAPTER TWO

The scroll, from the point of view of decipherment, could hardly have been opened at a worse place. We had entered, as it were, halfway through the story. The beginning lay embedded in the center of the larger, still unopened roll three thousand miles away in Jordan (Plate 6).

The writing at first sight looked remarkably clear. It had been punched out with a narrow stylus, perhaps no more than an eighth of an inch wide. The scribe had laid the sheets of metal onto a soft substance like wood and hammered his strokes fairly deeply into the copper, indenting sometimes as deep as the metal's original thickness. He had pegged down the right-hand edge of the scroll with some implement that had a square cross section, for when we finally reached the last segment, the blank right-hand margin had a quarter-of-an-inch hole drilled through about halfway down.

The scribe had certainly been no master of the art of engraving. Indeed, one glance at the segments in front of me showed that he had no intention of producing a work of beauty. He had simply to transfer to metal the text he had before him, written probably in a cursive hand and on strips of papyrus. And he was probably in a hurry.

To obtain a long line he made a number of small punch marks but failed often to connect them or to see that they lay in the same plane. A careful scribe working on parchment or papyrus would have ruled his sheets carefully first, both horizontally and vertically, and then hung his letters from the line (the resultant lining up of the tops of the letters in the scrolls makes photographs of scroll texts appear to the uninitiated to be upside down [*PDSS* Plates 50, 59–63]). Our engraver omitted to take this precaution, or to observe it, with the result that his lines of writing are anything but straight, and his letters vary considerably in size. Toward the bottom of the sheet they tend to become smaller as if his hands were working in a rather cramped position, and at the end of the whole document, as I discovered later, he seemed to become tired and his letters became smaller and punched with uneven pressure.

But if careless "penmanship" were the scribe's only fault, I should not have been unduly concerned. After all, not all the Dead Sea Scrolls are masterpieces of calligraphic art and we had become used to some very strange handwriting on the fragments we had been dealing with in Jerusalem. There were other difficulties and the first of these was evident from a glance at the very first line of writing. The scribe had extended his irregularity of layout to his word spacing, or rather his lack of it. It was not clear where one word ended and another began.

This was always a hazard in early Semitic writing and various means were taken to safeguard against misunderstanding on this account. Thus the Phoenicians and their literary successors, among whom were the Hebrews, divided their words with points. But in copying, these tended to be omitted and not a few of the difficulties we find in the text of the Bible stem from this fault. Later on as the more graceful Phoenician hand developed into the square Hebrew form that we most usually encounter in the scrolls, scribes began to finish words with an extra flourish on the last letter, or a prolongation of the final stroke. But not all the letters of the Hebrew alphabet lend themselves to this treatment, so that even at a late stage there was plenty of room for confusion if the words were not clearly separated.

Not only had our scribe's unskilled engraving failed to take adequate care in spacing his words, but for some reason he had confused his "medial" and "final" letters, almost as if deliberately trying to make the reading more difficult. This is a real possibility we shall have to consider later on when discussing the purpose of the document.

Now, these aberrancies would not have been so troublesome if I could have been sure that the scribe was writing the letters he really meant. But again, looking along the first line of script it was clear we had groups of consonants that just made no sense at all in Hebrew or any of its sister Semitic dialects. I then had to start juggling with the shape.

Some Hebrew letters of the alphabet look alike in even the most careful book hand, such as *w* and *y*, *b* and *k*, *d* and *r*, and so on, but our scribe, I found, had miswritten letters which one would have thought quite incapable of confusion, like *g* and *t* and even *'aleph*, the light Semitic glottal stop.

Furthermore, he had interspersed his square script here and there with cursive forms, a feature of the scroll which makes me think the scribe was copying from a cursively written document. A comparable fault in modern uneducated writing might be the mixing of small and capital letters, although there the difference would not be so marked as, for instance, when our scribe writes a cursive *'aleph* ⊂ for the normal square-shaped ⋉. Later on I discovered cases where his peculiarities in spelling resulted from careless pronunciation so that, as was becoming common at that time, certain gutturals became weakened to the point of their virtual disappearance in speech and so, as here, in writing.

The first word of the first line, however, made me realize that we had another problem to contend with: the scribe's vocabulary. On the whole the Dead Sea Scrolls have not posed too many problems in this regard. The language for the most part is biblical Hebrew, or a literary Aramaic for which we have a certain amount of inscriptional evidence. The purport of at least the first cache of scrolls was entirely religious, for which of course the Scriptures offer a rich treasury of words and phrases. But it was soon to become evident to me that our copper document was not a religious work in this sense and that its vocabulary was almost entirely composed of day-to-day words and expressions, many of which we do not find in the Bible at all, or only so rarely that their meaning is doubtful. Armed with the language of the Bible you could call down the wrath of God on an apostate city, or consign an erring king and his household to Sheol, but you would have difficulty in telling a gardener where to dig a ditch. Our scroll, as I was to discover, had very much to do with ditches, streams, wells, cisterns, and underground passages, and not at all with man's moral failings.

The first word of the segment I had cleaned read *shōbekh,* or something like it. Actually, even the vocalization of Hebrew at this period is uncertain for the only way to convey the vowels to the reader is by the use of certain consonants that have some vocalic affinity to the sounds required, like *w* for long *ō* or *ū*, *y* for long *ī* (*ee*). The short vowels are left mostly unrepresented. The first letter could as well be *s* as *sh* for only very much later was a point put above the letter to differentiate the two sibilants. As far as the Old Testament evidence goes we could read here either the name of an Aramaean general (II Sam. 10:16; in Chronicles, *Shōphākh*) or "a network of boughs" such as that which caused the downfall of the long-haired Absalom (II Sam. 18:9). Hebrew of a later period offers for this word "dovecot," probably connected with the root meaning of "latticework." Since the context favors something to do with water conduits, we can only suppose it had a special technical meaning like "sluice," which has otherwise not come down to us. This is the case with very many of the words in the copper scroll.

This segment offered another instance of a lost meaning to a word that must have been very common indeed among ordinary people. In the ninth line there is a word that is found only twice in the Old Testament and then with the quite different meanings of "tower" and "hole in the ground." It appeared eventually quite a number of times in the copper scroll and it was clear that there it again had a special reference, probably to some kind of rock-hewn tunnel.

In such rare words, of course, the would-be translator has recourse to other Semitic dialects like Aramaic or Arabic. But in the former case our literature is again of somewhat limited scope, although admittedly wider than biblical Hebrew; and in Arabic, although we have a vast literature, it is nearly all comparatively late, dating mostly from the time of the Muhammad in the seventh century of our era. It has therefore to be used with caution, even though in the past many

13

difficulties in our understanding of Old Testament words have been solved by recourse to this kindred dialect.

By the end of the day I had a few words down on a piece of paper, a lot more question marks, and a splitting headache. One thing was certain: this was no ordinary text of the kind we had so far seen in the scrolls. It was, as had been guessed previously, a catalogue of some kind. There were place names involved, like Beth Tamar, or the "Place of the Palms," and more detailed locations like water tanks, gutters, conduits, with directions referring to the cardinal points, and distances in cubits. There were sets of numerals preceded by the letters *kk*, and once the word for "silver" or "money."

Discussing the document with my wife, Joan, over supper that evening, I suggested that this word "silver" was probably the clue. The letters *kk* before the numerals could then be an abbreviation for *kikkarim* "talents." So it could be a list of monies due or paid, a kind of contract, but why, I asked, should places be specified in such detail?

"Let's have a look," she said, and scanned my translation for a moment. Then she handed it back with that infuriating look of intuitively acquired knowledge, characteristic of her sex.

"Yes, well, of course," she said, "it's a list of buried treasure."

CHAPTER THREE

My wife was not the first to suggest that the copper scroll was a treasure inventory. Soon after its discovery, a German professor, Karl Georg Kuhn, came to Jerusalem on a visit and asked permission of the museum authorities to study the unopened document (Plate 7). This was eventually granted, somewhat grudgingly, and with the minimum facilities. There exists in some academic circles a fierce regard for appropriated rights in the matter of unpublished texts that is redolent of the jungle. Kuhn was allowed to peer at the rolls through the glass of the showcases, but was not permitted to touch them nor have them removed from the case. Still he persevered, peering for hours on end at the side of the rolls he could see. Then he was lent photographs of their hidden undersides. He gleaned what he could from the indentations of letters and numerals just visible, and went away and wrote a paper suggesting that the copper scroll was an inventory of buried treasure.

I was working in the museum at the time on editing the parchment and papyrus scrolls, and well remember with what amusement Kuhn's suggestion was received by those who had the care of the document. The scrolls were producing many surprises, certainly. Almost daily, writings were appearing of whose existence we had known nothing, or which we had seen previously only in later translations. Some were even written in secret codes, but nothing quite so dramatic as a list of buried treasures had yet appeared.

Kuhn had supported his theory by pointing out that the Dead Sea Scrolls sect required that its initiates pool all their worldly wealth into a common fund. This was supervised by an official of the community called the overseer, and Kuhn suggested that the copper scroll was an inventory of this commonwealth which had been hidden away in the emergency that had brought the group's existence to an end.

Most scholars identified this communistic society with the Essenes of whom we had read previously in the works of the ancient historians. They had told us that about the time of Christ there existed a religious sect of the Jews who lived strictly disciplined lives, some of whom were celibates and had cut themselves off completely from the rest of the world in a monastic settlement by the Dead Sea. When the scrolls were found, archaeologists scoured the desert round about the Arab shepherd's cave for some other material remains of the people owning this fabulous library. About a mile to the south, on a plateau overlooking the sea, they had come across the ruins of some buildings which exploratory soundings soon showed to have been in use over the turn of our era (Plate 8). Pottery found there corresponded with that recovered from the cave and it seemed reasonable to assume that there was some connection between them. After five seasons' excavation it is now possible to walk through the rooms and climb up onto the watchtower and down into the great plastered cisterns of the settlement, or "monastery." Most people believe that this was the home of the Scrolls sect and that in a room where writing benches and inkwells were found, many of the Dead Sea Scrolls were written.

The name of the place is known locally as Khirbet ("ruins of") Qumran, pronounced *kumrahn* or *gumrahn*. By the side of the settlement a dry river valley, called the Wadi Qumran, winds its way from the great cliffs to the sea.

Coins found in and about the monastery showed that it had been inhabited from about 100 B.C. down to the second year of the first great Jewish Revolt against the Romans, that is, A.D. 68. In the early summer of that year the Roman general, Vespasian, reached Jericho in his march south to crush the center of the revolt in Jerusalem. It seems likely that he cleared out the little Jewish settlement at Qumran at this time. You can today pick up pieces of charred wood among the ruins which tell the sad story of the end of the settlement, and the archaeologists found Roman arrowheads among the embers which showed that at the end the place had not been undefended.

But even in its heyday, the Qumran establishment was a very crudely built affair. There are few examples of worked masonry in the buildings which are mainly constructed of large pieces of rock laid one on top of the other and plastered in position. There arc, it is true, several pillar drums and bases lying about, one of them only partly finished (*PDSS* Plates 160, 161), but none is in position and how it was intended to fit them into the existing rudimentary architecture it is difficult to see. For the monastery was to the Jews of Qumran no lasting city: they longed for the day when, led by their Messiah or Christ, they could return over the hills to a purified Jerusalem and begin the promised millennium of peace and plenty. It is, of course, this fevered anticipation of the coming of the Kingdom and the Christ that makes their works such interesting reading to students of the New Testament.

Qumran, then, is not the kind of place where one would expect to find lists of buried treasure, but from the look of those first two opened segments of the copper scroll, it seemed that Kuhn was to be wonderfully vindicated against the skeptics. I returned to the College of Science and Technology the next morning eager to see what the next pieces might reveal.

The second segment had included the first letters of the next column of script, but the next cut we arranged to pass very neatly through a margin, leaving only one letter of the column outside. Baker was now becoming practiced in the gentle art of scroll sawing and eventually reduced the actual cutting time from ten to two-and-a-half minutes. After each cut and removal of the segment, the dust still clinging to the body of the roll was scraped and brushed away and then a coat of adhesive applied to the newly revealed surface. The roll could then be put into an electric oven for an hour or two and baked, while the work of cleaning the segment proceeded.

Although a painter's ordinary soft brush sufficed for most of the dust on the face of the segment, we later imported from the University Dental School a dentist's drill, into the revolving end of which could be slotted tiny nylon-tufted brushes. These lifted the dust from the crevices very efficiently and avoided putting undue pressure on the fragile substance of the scroll (Plate 9). Baker also used this instrument with its full complement of drills and grinding heads to remove the plaster packing and particularly stubborn patches of hardened material adhering to the surface. It was all very effective but it put my teeth on edge the whole time. Later on the Dental School claimed their machine back for another kind of operational use, and the "Tech." bought one for themselves. They have not, as

18

far as I know, opened up their own dental clinic yet, and if they do I shall not be among the first customers.

The next column confirmed my wife's judgment on the scroll. Treasure was indeed involved, and in such quantities that it took my breath away.

The sixth and seventh lines spoke of "sixty-two talents of silver" and the tenth and eleventh lines, of "three hundred talents of gold." In both cases the word for "talents" was here written in full.

This segment offered more locations, including the place names of the Great Wadi and Beth Kerem, or "House of the Vineyard." Line twelve also spoke of "the monument of Absalom" where eighty talents were buried twelve cubits down on the western side.

This seemed to be the general format of the inventory. Each paragraph began a new item which would start with a general location within a larger reference which is then stated, followed by more details on the actual positioning of the cache, thus:

In the reservoir which is in Beth Kerem, ten cubits on its left as you enter: sixty-two talents of silver.

A "cubit" can be roughly taken as eighteen inches, so if we knew where the reservoir of Beth Kerem was, we would have little difficulty in locating the treasure hiding place. But the "if" is a large one, not only in this case but, as we shall see, in many other sites of the scroll's topography.

In little more than a week the roll was open. Toward the center, of course, the segments became narrower and some breakage occurred, on the very last piece particularly. The fragments were reassembled without too much difficulty, however, and fastened in position with Durofix and strapped across the breaks with strips of Perspex.

Immediately I had grasped the purport of the scroll and was reasonably certain of the text I wrote to Harding in Jordan, and followed that brief communication in November with a full transcript of the text, a provisional translation, and notes. But the beginning of the scroll we had still to see, and I urged Harding to expedite the sending of the second, larger roll as soon as possible. It was not until the end of the year that he could obtain permission from the authorities to let it come. He told me later that he had booked a seat in a plane to London for his Arab assistant before he had the signed authority in his hand. This he had to obtain from the Cabinet Minister concerned and was so much delayed that he finally received it from the official's hands only an hour or so before the plane was due to leave. With the ink on the document still wet, and lacking the countersignature of the Prime Minister as the law really required, Harding dashed from the office, grabbed his assistant clutching the scroll, and motored at breakneck speed to the airport, arriving with minutes to spare.

The precious roll arrived in Manchester on 2 January. Wright Baker was away on holiday at the time and we had to tour Manchester looking for his private bank to lodge the scroll in a safe deposit. However, when eventually work began the cutting went smoothly and even more quickly than the first part. By nine o'clock on the evening of 16 January, the final piece came away. All twelve columns of script now lay open after their two-thousand-year-old concealment (Plate 10). There was no title, but the first item referred to a place name which was exciting enough, for it lay very close to Qumran.

Here is my translation, still full of uncertainties and only very tentative in many places, but enough, I think, to let us take our story a stage further. The specialist will find a complete facsimile and transcription of the Hebrew text in the first edition of this book, pages 32–55.

Item 1. In the fortress which is in the Vale of Achor, forty cubits under the steps entering to the east: a money chest and its contents, of a weight of seventeen talents. KϵN.

Item 2. In the sepulchral monument, in the third course of stones: 100 bars of gold.

Item 3. In the Great Cistern which is in the Court of the Peristyle, in the spout in its floor, concealed in a hole in front of the upper opening: nine hundred talents.

Item 4. In the mound of KHLT: tithe vessels, consisting of *lôg* measures and amphorae, all of tithe and stored Seventh Year produce and Second Tithe of rejected offerings (*piggul*). Its opening is in the trough of the water conduit, six cubits from the north toward the hewn immersion pool. XAΓ.

Item 5. In the ascent of the escape staircase, in the left-hand side, three cubits up from the floor: forty talents of [sil]ver.

Item 6. In the salt pit which is under the steps: 42 talents. HN.

Item 7. In the cavity of the Old House of Tribute, in the Chain Platform: sixty-five bars of gold. Θϵ.

Item 8. In the cistern that is within the underground passage which is in the Court of Wood Stores there are vessels and seventy talents of silver.

Item 9. In the cistern which is nineteen cubits in front of the eastern gateway, there are vessels, and in the irrigation channel that is in it: ten talents. ΔI.

Item 10. In the cistern that is under the wall on the east, in a spur of rock: six pitchers of silver; its entrance is under the Great Threshold.

Item 11. In the pool which is in the east of KHLT, buried at one cubit, four *sit's* in the northern corner: 22 talents.

Item 12. In the C[ourt of . . .], nine cubits under the southern corner: gold and silver vessels for tithe, sprinkling basins, cups, sacrificial bowls, libation vessels; in all, six hundred and nine.

Item 13. Under the other, eastern corner, buried at sixteen cubits: 40 talents of silver. TP.

Item 14. In the pit which is to the north of the Esplanade tithe vessels and garments. Its entrance is under the western corner.

Item 15. In the tomb which is to the northeast of the Esplanade, three cubits under the corpse: 13 talents.

Item 16. In the Great Cistern which is in [. . .], in a pillar in its north: [. . .] talents. ΣK.

Item 17. In the water conduit which enters [. . .] as you go in four [. . .] cubits: 40 talents of silver [in] a chest (?).

Item 18. Between the two buildings (?) that are in the Vale of Achor, midway between them, buried at three cubits, there (are hidden) two pots filled with silver.

Item 19. In the clay pit which is trough of the [. . .]: two hundred talents of silver.

Item 20. In the eastern pit which is in the north of KHLT: seventy talents of silver.

Item 21. In the dam (?) that is in the Valley of Secacah, buried at one cubit: 12 talents of silver.

Item 22. At the head of the water conduit [which penetrates (?)] Secacah from the north, buried th[ree] cubits under the great [. . .]: 7 talents of silver.

Item 23. In the fissure that is in Secacah, in the spo[ut (?)] of the "Solomon" reservoir: tithe vessels arranged side by side (?).

Item 24. Sixty cubits from the "Solomon" aqueduct toward the great watchtower, buried at three cubits: 23 talents of silver.

Item 25. In the tomb which is in the Wadi *Kippā'*, on the way from Jericho to Secacah, buried at seven cubits: 32 talents.

Item 26. [In] the cavity of the pillar of the Double Gate, facing east, [in] the northern entrance, buried at three [cu]bits, (hidden) there is a pitcher; in it, one scroll, under it 42 talents.

Item 27. In the cavity at the base of the watchtower that faces east, buried in the entrance at nine cubits: 21 talents.

Item 28. In the Tomb of the Queen, in the western side, buried at twelve cubits: 7½ talents.

Item 29. In the dam (?) which is in the Bridge of the High Priest [. . .] nine [cubits (?)]: [. . .] talents.

Item 30. In the water conduit of [. . .] the north[ern] reservoir in four [. . .] a distance of twenty cubits, fo[ur *sît's* (?)]: four hundred talents.

Item 31. In the recess which is adjacent to the cool room of the Summer House, buried at six cubits: six pitchers of silver.

Item 32. In Dōk, under the eastern corner of the guardhouse, buried at seven cubits: 22 talents.

Item 33. By the mouth of the water out**let** of Kozibah, buried three cubits toward the overflow **tank**: 80 talents of gold in two pitchers.

Item 34. [In the drain]pipe which is in the eastern path to the Treasury, which is east of the Entrance: tithe jars and scrolls in among the jars.

Item 35. In the Outer Valley, in the middle of the circle (?) upon (or, by) the Stone, buried at seventeen cubits under it: 17 talents of silver and gold.

Item 36. In the dam (?) at the mouth of the Kidron gorge, buried at three cubits: 7 talents.

Item 37. In the stubble field of the Shaveh, facing southwest, in an underground passage looking north, buried at twenty-four cubits: 67 talents.

Item 38. In the irrigation channel (?) of the Shaveh, in the constricted part (?) that is in it, buried at eleven cubits: 70 talents of silver.

Item 39. In the sluice (?) which is in the bottom of the rainwater tank, buried at a distance of three cubits and two (*sît's?*) from its bottom, in the plaster lining the sides: four staters.

Item 40. In the Second Enclosure, in the underground passage that faces east, buried at eight and a half cubits: 23½ talents.

Item 41. In the underground passages of The Hollows (?), in the passage facing south, buried in the spout at sixteen cubits: 22 talents.

Item 42. In the funnel, much silver of the freewill offering.

Item 43. In the pipe of waters that run to the trough of the drain, buried seven cubits from the outside toward their mouth: 9 talents.

Item 44. In the ditch that is to the north of the mouth of the gorge of the Place of the Palms (Beth Tamar), at the outlet of the Valley of PL', everything in it is consecrated offering (*hērem*).

Item 45. In the sluice (?) that is in the stronghold of [. . .] south, in the second story as it runs down from above: 9 talents.

Item 46. In the cistern which is alongside the irrigation channels that are fed from the Great Wadi; in its floor: 12 talents.

Item 47. In the reservoir which is in the Place of the Vineyard, (Beth Kerem), ten cubits on its left as you enter: sixty-two talents of silver.

Item 48. In the basin of the Valley of [. . .], in its western side (there is) a sealing stone of two cubits: it is the opening: three hundred talents of gold and ten serving vessels.

Item 49. Under the Monument of Absalom, on the western side, buried at twelve cubits: 80 talents.

Item 50. In the basin of the Bathhouse of Black Marble (?), under the gutter: 17 talents.

Item 51. [In the . . .], in its four inner corner buttresses: tithe vessels, arranged side by side (?).

Item 52. Below the Portico's southern corner, in the Tomb of Zadok, under the pillar of the exedra: vessels of tithe of [. . .] and tithe of [. . .], arranged side by side (?).

Item 53. In the treading place (?) at the top of the cliff facing west, in front of the Garden of Zadok, under the great sealing stone that is in its outlet: consecrated offerings (*hērem*).

Item 54. In the tomb which is under the paving stones (?): 40 talents.

Item 55. In the grave of the common people of pure life (?); there are vessels of tithe or tithe of [. . .], arranged side by side (?).

Item 56. In the House of the Twin Pools (Bethesda?), in the pool as you approach its settling basins: vessels of tithe of [. . .] and tithe of [. . .], arranged side by side (?).

Item 57. In the entrance of the western lod[ging (?)] of the House of Rest, is a base for a portable stove beside [. . .]: nine hundred [vessels (?)], five talents of gold, sixty talents (of silver); its entrance is from the west. Under the black stone are juglets. Under the sill of the cistern are 42 talents.

Item 58. In Mount Gerizim, under the ascent of its upper ditch: one chest and its contents, and 60 talents of silver.

Item 59. In the mouth of the spring of the Temple (?): vessels of silver and vessels of gold for tithe and silver, the whole being six hundred talents.

Item 60. In the Great Drain of the Basin: vessels of the House of the Basin, the whole having a weight of 71 talents, twenty minas.

Item 61. In a pit adjoining on the north, in a hole opening northward, and buried at its mouth: a copy of this document, with an explanation and their measurements, and an inventory of each and every thing.

CHAPTER FOUR

As soon as I had made a reasonably complete, though still very tentative translation of the second part of the scroll, I sent it, with the transcribed Hebrew and notes, to Harding in Amman. It was never acknowledged, but not altogether surprisingly for by this time a most strange atmosphere of secrecy and even churlishness had enveloped our work.

At the beginning of January I had occasion to give a series of three broadcasts on the BBC on the Dead Sea Scrolls generally. A great deal of wild conjecture about the possible influence of the Essenes on Jesus of Nazareth had been current just previously, and something I said about the possibility of the Essene leader's also having been crucified apparently stirred the imagination of some elements of the press and caused alarm in religious circles. My colleagues in Jerusalem, fearful for the effect this "revelation" might have upon the faithful, strenuously denied the possibility of the Essene leader's crucifixion, and wrote a joint letter of dissent to the London *Times*. Whatever comfort this may have offered the laity, this apparent "rift" between members of the scrolls editing team was pounced upon in some quarters as evidence that somebody somewhere was trying to conceal matters which might affect religious vested interests, a suspicion already voiced by some popular writers. Rather more realistically, it was also made plain to the world that

I did not feel myself bound by ecclesiastical or other ties to follow any "party line" in my interpretation of the scrolls.

Of course, in all this the copper scroll was not concerned. I realized that the first news of its contents should be made centrally, probably from Jordan, and I daily awaited the release that would satisfy the constant stream of inquiries I was receiving from all over the world. Naturally, once scholars knew that this mysterious text had been opened and read they were eager to learn its contents, for research in the scrolls and their influence upon Jewish and Christian developments was at its height, particularly on the Continent and in the United States. Any new piece of information was seized upon avidly, and articles and books were even being written on the basis of only rumored contents of newly discovered documents.

But complete silence ensued. Then, in Manchester, the generally happy atmosphere in the "Tech." laboratory suddenly chilled. On one occasion I arrived at the college to be sternly "rebuked" by my colleague for having allowed a neighbor of mine to develop some photographs I had taken of the work of cutting the scroll. On another occasion, I was even reprimanded for having let slip to the press that we were having to cut it open since the copper was too oxidized to unroll, as self-evident and innocent a piece of information as one could imagine. Visitors, even the principal of the college, were received in the laboratory, if at all, with ill grace.

All this I noted with amused bewilderment, but went on with my work on the text, thinking that perhaps the focusing of world interest on our work was inducing those concerned to overdramatize the situation. Even when Professor Baker gave a lecture in

Manchester on the opening of the scroll, the manner of which had apparently by then been cleared for publication by the Jerusalem authorities, and sternly warned me to keep away lest I should be pressed for information on the contents, I merely shrugged it off. I was still expecting an official release of information that would bring the matter into a proper perspective.

Yet nothing happened, and in fact it was not until six months after our opening of the scroll and its first decipherment that the release was made. The first I knew of it was a telephone call from a press agency asking me to confirm the news of the scroll's contents which had just been given to the world by the Professor of Mechanical Engineering. He had been sent from Jordan a copy of the notice which was to be issued simultaneously to the press in the United States, France, and Britain. A few days later I received a letter from Amman telling me that this was the "official" view of the document, and twelve days after the release, Baker sent me a similar letter enclosing his own expanded version of the official statement. This included his notes on the Essene library from Qumran, for, as he said, he "didn't want the public to get away with the notion that the Essenes were just gold hoarders."

The purport of this official statement was that the copper scroll treasure inventory was a kind of fairy tale, completely legendary and on no account to be treated as factual. It included translations of three items which were, to say the least, debatable, and chosen presumably to underline the supposed unrealistic tenor of the document.

Now this estimate of the scroll is, of course, quite legitimate. I do not myself share it, and I cannot think that in the face of all the evidence of the text itself many scholars will. But it seemed to me an extraordinary action on the part of my Jerusalem colleagues to make such a dogmatic statement to the public on a matter which would have to be the subject of scholarly debate for many years. However, I kept my peace and rejoiced in the one element which was entirely welcome, that the official publication of this most important document was to be put into the hands of my friend and colleague, Father Joseph Milik.

Milik is perhaps the most brilliant of our little team of scroll editors (Plate 11). He had left his native Poland after the war as a very young man, taken orders as a secular priest of the Roman Church, and gone to Rome to complete his theological training. There he showed strong promise as a scholar of Semitic languages, and published from Rome papers on the Qumran documents that brought him to the attention of Father de Vaux of the French Biblical School in Jerusalem. He was invited there to take part in the editing of the scroll fragments found in the first cave and subsequently became a founder-member of our editing team dealing with the mass of documentary material discovered in 1952. He developed an extraordinary facility for reading Semitic scripts of a cursive character never before seen, and for recognizing the work of individual scribes from the tiniest fragments, which is the basis of our work of piecing together the torn scrolls into their original documents. His continual residence in Jerusalem while engaged on this work enabled him to act as a willing adviser to those of us who could only come for broken periods.

Milik has a delightful sense of humor, and early on, to my joy, I found that he shared my affection for the literary progeny of that master-humorist, P. G. Wodehouse. Our "Scrollery" conversation became larded with Woosterisms and Gussie Fink-Nottleisms that were the despair of our companions.

Of all the Jerusalem team, Milik was certainly the best fitted to carry the initial decipherment of the copper scroll a stage further, and since he had been one of the party that had taken part in the search that had found the scroll, it was doubly fitting that he should be entrusted with its edition for the definitive publication. I hoped that this would not be long delayed, particularly in view of the dubious nature of the public statement and the manner of its release.

Very soon after, Gerald Harding was relieved of his post as Director of Antiquities, and a Jordanian official appointed in his place. Later, in 1957, when I visited Jordan to carry on my work of editing the scroll fragments, I took the opportunity of continuing my studies of the copper scroll, which was now lying open to public view in the small Jordan Museum in Amman.

I discovered to my astonishment that the new Director had not been given a translation of the document. He had presumably not seen my correspondence with Harding, and of course, quite naturally was very anxious to know the scroll's contents. There seemed to have developed a hostile atmosphere between the Department of Antiquities and the Palestine Museum and its trustees, which in view of this secretive attitude over a piece of Jordan's property was not entirely surprising. It was further aggravated by the prevailing political situation in which Western interests in Jordan, which included the Palestine Archaeological Museum, were viewed with growing hostility. This air of distrust was not relieved by the attitude of the museum toward the Arab officials, illustrated by the words of a prominent member of the trustees when telling me not to give a translation of

33

the copper scroll's contents to the Director of Antiquities because "you simply can't trust them with the information."

The Department had nobody on its staff conversant with Hebrew so that it depended entirely on foreign scholars for its knowledge of the scrolls. The Director and staff offered every possible facility for the work of studying them in their country and naturally expected in return a frankness about their contents and significance that would enable them to estimate their value to their country. It was largely due to Gerald Harding's ability to bridge the gap between scholars and government that resulted in Jordan's allotting £15,000 in 1952 from its very meager treasury to rescue scroll fragments from a fresh discovery at Qumran.

I considered this secretive attitude on the part of the Western archaeologists at the museum both shortsighted and dangerous. Apparently they were afraid that the publication of a list of buried treasure might start a gold rush throughout Palestine that could endanger archaeological sites. It seemed to me that they had let this fear overweigh their judgment to the point of jeopardizing still further the already shaken confidence of the Jordan Government in the friendly intentions of their advisers and, what was worse, were giving the public added grounds for believing that they could, if occasion demanded, suppress information from the scrolls. When documents were being found that were already seriously influencing opinion on matters of such emotional import as the origins and uniqueness of Christianity, any further hint of suppression or delay in publication, for whatever reason, could only arouse the gravest apprehension. Furthermore, scholars all over the world were being left in an impossible situation, realizing that an important document was lying in Jordan, its contents known only to a handful of people, and being apparently expected to remain content with some trifling press release containing little hard information of any consequence coupled with an obviously one-sided view of the scroll's significance.

I resisted all attempts to make an early publication of my views on the document until the authorities had published the full text. This, I thought, could not be long delayed. It was inconceivable that it should be held back until the definitive volume appeared, many years hence. However, when I pressed the need for an earlier publication, the answer was returned that since that particular volume of the series would otherwise be deficient in interesting material, the copper scroll must be held back to give the book added substance, a point of view hardly likely to commend itself to scholars whose researches were being seriously hampered for lack of authoritative information.

The new Director of Antiquities offered me every facility for continuing my study of the text. I was also enabled to make two complete sets of photographs of the face of the scroll. This was a long and tedious process, for the curve in its surface meant that each segment had to be photographed many times in slightly different positions. The Director also gave me full rights to make my own publication of the text, denying vehemently that Milik or any of the museum personnel had permission to do so. However, I had no wish to aggravate the already delicate situation existing between the department and the museum and merely conveyed the information to the doyen of the museum trustees.

The situation now prevailing in the editing team was far from happy. For my part, I had pushed the disclaimer to the *Times* out of my mind. During a visit to Britain by de Vaux, the editor in chief, and chief signatory of the letter, I had met him at a congress on Old Testament studies and talked amicably with him much as usual. He had, without prompting, assured me that the idea of writing the letter had come from "the others" and not from himself. A letter from one of my American colleagues, a Jesuit priest, had apologized for believing it necessary to subscribe to the disclaimer but he felt he had a responsibility to his lay charges to set their minds at rest. I went to Jerusalem that summer resolved not to allow the wretched affair to cloud my previously happy relationships with my colleagues.

But I had not been long in the museum before realizing with sinking heart that our relations were not to be allowed to recover their old happy state. Even my friend Milik had clearly been instructed by his superiors not to discuss the scrolls with me more than necessary and least of all the copper document. I believe Milik felt as unhappy about the situation as I, for our relationship had always been of the most open hitherto, and our conversation quite unfettered by the dictates of his priestly office. We had talked in the past very frankly indeed about such questions as the historical basis for Christian beliefs, and he had never hesitated to discuss with extreme candor the direction in which his own unbiased researches in the scrolls seemed to be leading. However, his ability to continue his work in Jerusalem depended on the good will and support of persons not quite so liberal in their views and he apparently had no option but to obey their dictates regarding myself.

I went home after that summer's work in Jordan to continue my own researches into the text and topography of the scroll, becoming more and more convinced that to treat it as the work of a madman and a mere collection of baseless legends was to miss its importance that extended far beyond the treasure it listed. Arrangements were made for my own studies to be published in the predecessor of this book, but sufficiently far in the future to allow Milik to propagate the "official" view and support it with as much evidence as he could muster. In fact, the definitive volume was so delayed that my book appeared first. Knowing that it was well on its way in the press, Milik was induced, I think unwisely, to publish a complete translation of the text of the scroll in a learned French journal without the Hebrew to support his readings. Far from helping other scholars to come to grips with the many problems presented by the document, such a partial presentation after all the delay merely added insult to injury. It was all rather childish and helped nobody.

Now, at last, however, Milik's definitive version has appeared, and in the foregoing translation I have been able to utilize his work in revising my initial decipherment. We still differ in a number of points of detail, but in not a few instances I have felt that his choice of alternatives has the edge of probability, and specialists can see in most cases where I have followed his judgment. As always, his scholarship is impeccable and he has been able to bring to the linguistic and topographical problems of the scroll a breadth of knowledge that is remarkable in such a comparatively young man.

Yet, he still apparently clings to the belief that the inventory is basically fictitious, although he is compelled to acknowledge that the author of this "fairy tale" has contrived to give his work a remarkable appearance of reality. We must presume that this is Milik's own uninfluenced judgment and must therefore spend a moment or two looking at this legendary genre of Jewish literature with which he associates our copper scroll.

CHAPTER FIVE

Tales of buried treasure are to be found in any folklore, and Jewish literature has them in full measure. There they largely concern the fabulous wealth of King Solomon and the Temple he built. The Bible dwells lovingly on the splendor of this building, lavishly equipped in all respects, and the pride of its chief architect (I Kings 6). Its double doorway, some fifteen feet wide, was inlaid with gold, as were the walls, which were paneled with cedar and engraved with palm trees, open flowers, chains, and cherubim. Around the main hall were placed items of sacred furniture: the golden candlesticks, the table for the shewbread, and a small cedarwood altar overlaid in gold leaf. In the innermost sanctum, the Holy of Holies, stood the great olivewood cherubim, fifteen feet high and sheathed in gold, guarding the Temple's most sacred possession, the Ark of the Covenant. This was a wooden box, said to contain the two stone tablets engraved with the Ten Commandments. The sacred utensils included shovels and fleshhooks, tongs, cups, snuffers, basins, spoons, and fire-pans, most of which had their equivalents in the later Temple in existence at the time of our scroll (cf. Item 12).

Solomon's Temple was destroyed by the Assyrian armies of Nebuchadnezzar in the sixth century B.C., and the disposal of its wealth forms the basis of many a legend, handed down from generation to generation.

The Second Book of the Maccabees, for example, makes Jeremiah the chief custodian of the treasure after the fall of Jerusalem. Following a divine warning, the prophet "commanded the Tabernacle and the Ark to accompany him" and went to Mount Nebo on the eastern side of the Dead Sea. There he found a cave in which he placed the Tabernacle, the Ark, and the incense altar, and then sealed its entrance. Even the prophet's followers did not know its whereabouts, but he promised that it would be revealed when "God [shall] gather his people again together, and receive them unto mercy" (II Macc. 2:4–8). Another version elaborates the story still further: only Aaron would bring forth the Ark, and only Moses would be allowed to touch the stone tablets inside. The location of the cave is here specified as "between the two mountains on which Moses and Aaron lay buried."

Other traditions reckoned, perhaps more realistically, on the treasure being carried off to Mesopotamia with the Jewish exiles, or buried on the site of the Temple itself. Thus the seven-branched candlestick and seventy-seven golden tables were among those pieces hidden in a tower in Baghdad. A scribe is said to have found there jewels, pearls, gold, and silver and handed them over to an angel, who hid them in Borsippa. The sacred musical instruments were in the charge of Baruch and Zedekiah. Some sacred vessels were believed to lie under a stone by Daniel's grave in Shushan. Whoever touched the stone fell dead, and a similar fate awaited any archaeologist who dared to excavate the area.

On the other hand, the Apocalypse of Baruch tells us that an angel descended from heaven into the Holy of Holies and took the Veil of the Altar, the Ark, the Mercy Seat, two tables, the incense altar, and the forty-eight precious jewels with which the high priest was adorned, and all the holy vessels of the Tabernacle and commanded the earth to open and swallow them up (II Bar. 6:7–10). The Temple gates were also said to have descended miraculously into the earth; another legend of the Jeremiah cycle makes the prophet conceal the high-priestly gown of Aaron under the cornerstone of the Sanctuary, by which may be meant the rock upon which the Altar itself stood.

King Josiah is also credited with hiding some sacred objects, including the Ark, an earthen vessel filled with manna, a jar of oil used by Moses for anointing the sacred implements, pitchers of water from Miriam's well, Aaron's rod, and a coffer containing the offerings of the Philistines.

Most of these traditions look to the time when the Messiah would restore the glory of the Temple and its treasures. One version has it that a river would flow out of the Holy of Holies all the way to the Euphrates, uncovering the treasure deposits as it went.

The Samaritans, too, had their own Temple and their share of treasure legend. The Samaritan Sanctuary on Mount Gerizim was destroyed by the Jewish priest-king John Hyrcanus (135–104 B.C.), and they believed that its treasure was hidden nearby. One day their Messiah would come and restore it to them, and Josephus records an incident in Pontius Pilate's troubled governorship, when a messianic pretender gathered a large crowd of followers about him on the promise of showing them where the treasures were concealed (JA XVIII iv 1; §85 f.).

Another fruitful source of treasure legends has been the supposed rich burials of the ancient Israelite kings. David's tomb, in particular, seems to have served as a never-failing nest egg for penurious rulers. John Hyrcanus made off with three thousand talents from this tomb, we are told (JA XIII viii 4; §249), and Herod the Great was deterred from completing its pillage only by some kind of heavenly flame thrower (JA XVI vii 1; §179 f.).

All such stories bear the obvious marks of fiction either in the manner and place of concealment or in the nature of the treasure concerned. They are mentioned here only because these are the kind of fairy tales that have been seriously compared with the copper scroll. Yet, the realistic nature of the treasure concerned here (lacking, it will be noticed, all reference to the Ark, the shewbread tables, and even the seven-branched candlestick), and of the places of concealment, should have distinguished our document clearly from this legendary genre of literature.

At first sight, the amounts of treasure recorded in the copper scroll might seem fantastic, but these, I believe, can be reasonably explained. Totals of precious metals concerned (as far as the text can now be read) are as follows:

Silver (including mixed gold and silver and weights of unspecified materials): 3179+ talents, 20 minas, and 4 staters.
Gold: 385 talents.
Gold Bars: 165+ in number.
Pitchers Containing Silver: 14 in number.
Vessels Made of Silver and Gold: 619 in number.

Whether these amounts are abnormally large depends, of course, on the weight we accord the talent of this period. If it be as high as that obtaining, for example, in contemporary rabbinic literature, about 45 pounds, then we arrive at such colossal totals as 64 tons of silver and 8 tons of gold! Even more absurd would be an estimate based on probable values of the talent in Old Testament times, giving something in the order of 134 tons of precious metal. However, a closer examination of the text will show that such values are out of the question, if only that the two water pitchers of Item 33, with their "eighty talents" of gold, would have to be of a size capable of holding one and a half tons between them! A further striking discrepancy among such vast amounts would be the four coins called "staters" hidden in the plaster lining the sides of a rainwater sluice (Item 39). Each of these coins was the equivalent of the "half-shekel" of Matthew 17:24.

The fact is that we have no certain knowledge what values were accorded the talent and its factors in Judaean common speech of the first century. It must often have occurred to readers of the New Testament that the amounts usually credited by commentaries to the talents of Jesus' parables seemed abnormally large. The unjust steward (Matt. 18:23 f.), for instance, could have held his own quite comfortably on Wall Street as far as his material resources were concerned, and the "good and faithful servant" who speculated so successfully with his five talents would have needed a fair-sized wheelbarrow to bring his master the resultant four hundredweights of silver (Matt. 25:14 f.).

In II Maccabees and Josephus we find the same kind of amounts quoted for the Temple treasures. Thus Antiochus Epiphanes "carried out of the Temple a thousand eight hundred talents" (II Macc. 5:21), and the pillaging of the Temple treasury by Crassus

amounted to two thousand talents which Pompey had left, and he was prepared to strip the sanctuary of all its gold, which amounted to eight thousand talents. He also took a bar of solid beaten gold, weighing three hundred minas (JA XIV vii 1; §105 f.).

Perhaps we come nearer a true understanding of these amounts in Josephus, the New Testament, and our scroll if we downgrade the official "talent" to the value of the next denomination, the *maneh* (Greek *mina*), the sixtieth part of a talent, and the *maneh* to the shekel, a fiftieth part of the *maneh*. Josephus does much the same when he loosely equates the *maneh* with the shekel in recounting the story of Joseph and his sale to the Ishmaelites (Gen. 37:28; JA II iii 3; §33).

There is other evidence for a similar regionalization of monetary values at this time, for we read that the Galilean *sela'* was reckoned as only half the Judaean value for this coin. We may, perhaps, compare the English slang "dollar" for five shillings, and even more appositely, the semi-jocular substitution of "pound" for "shilling" and "shilling" for "penny" among British tradesmen, omnibus conductors, and the like.

All one can say for certain is that this supposition gives very reasonable amounts for the treasure deposits of our scroll. A rather interesting piece of confirmatory evidence may be found in an actual treasure deposit within the Qumran monastery. Under the plaster floor of one of the rooms (Figure 6; *PDSS* Plates 173, 174) was found a treasure hoard of 558 Tyrian tetradrachmae whose weight was something in the region of fifteen pounds (see Chapter Seven). The coins had been carefully hidden away in three small juglets, sealed with fiber stoppers. They do not seem to be among the Qumran items listed on the scroll, but may conceivably be connected with such treasure deposits. In any case, the size of this cache does coincide rather well with the average of the scroll items, estimated as above.

Reading, then, our scroll "talent" as a *maneh* of twelve ounces, we may estimate the totals as follows:

> *Silver:* 21 cwt.
> *Gold:* 2½ cwt.

To this one should add the unspecified weight of gold bars, money-filled pitchers, and gold and silver vessels.

Great as this wealth was, there is reason to believe that it was not for its monetary value alone that the treasure was hidden away. A number of the items make no mention of weight or value; indeed, some would have no monetary worth whatsoever. Of such would be the "tithe" of various kinds and "tithe vessels" which were in some cases apparently quite empty (cf. Item 4). These items really hold the clue to our treasure scroll, and to understand their significance we must digress a little into the subject of Jewish tithes and tax obligations.

The basis of the Temple economics was the annual half-shekel poll tax, levied not only in Palestine but throughout the Jewish Dispersion (Exod. 30:13, 38:26; Matt. 17:24). From Jewish communities in every part of the civilized world these dues poured into the Jerusalem Temple, and many pious Jews donated, in addition, private freewill offerings (JA XIV vii 2; §110 f.). This money was used for the upkeep of the Temple and its services and was kept until needed in the Temple treasuries, which also acted as a kind of savings bank for the city's inhabitants, rich and poor alike (II Macc. 3:6 f.; JW VI v 2; §282). Despite numerous plunderings of these deposits by needy rulers, native and foreign, the wealth of the Temple grew to vast proportions and became proverbial.

Apart from the poll tax, however, the priests officiating in private sacrifices were allowed a share of the offering, and the hundreds of lesser clergy who performed the menial duties in the Temple rituals were maintained by a system of religious taxation. The basis of this system was a tithe of agricultural produce, which included "anything that is used for food, and is kept watch over and grows from the soil" (cf. Num. 18; Matt. 23:23; Luke 11:42). Added to this first tithe, there was a "Second Tithe" (cf. Item 4) of the same produce, which together with a cattle tithe (Lev. 27:32 f.) furnished a feast for the owner and his guests in Jerusalem (Deut. 14:22–27). Then, every third year, a "poor tithe" was levied for charity (Deut. 14:28 f., 26:12). The first fruits of grain and fruit crops were also considered the priests' due, and the biblical passage that commands it (Num. 18:12 f.) makes it clear that such offerings belong by right to God and are sacred. He ceded His rights over them to His priests, but until these first fruits had been offered to God, the crop might not be used by men in any way (Lev. 23:14).

So it was for any produce, or its equivalent in money, that had been set aside as tithe: it was holy and conveyed in itself or anything it touched that special quality of sanctity which made it dangerous for any but priests to handle. To use such goods for non-religious purposes was a heinous sin, for it was *hērem*, "consecrated offering" (cf. Items 44, 53), or *qorbān* (Matt. 27:6; Mark 7:11).

Pontius Pilate incurred the wrath of the Jewish priesthood by using such money from the Temple coffers to build or rebuild an aqueduct bringing much needed water from Etan, south of Bethlehem, to Jerusalem (Figure 2). The scheme was a worthy one, but the use of Temple tribute for this secular purpose was unlawful in the eyes of the Temple hierarchy and stirred up against that luckless Roman governor even greater animosity than usual (JA XVIII iii 2; §60 f.). Furthermore, it was laid down that when a city was about to be destroyed, all dedicated things in it must first be redeemed for money and the tithe allowed to rot, as being "spoil belonging to Heaven." The Second Tithe (cf. Item 4) and the sacred Scriptures (cf. Items 26, 34) "must be hidden away." Responsibility for clearly designating this hidden consecrated offering lay with the concealer, and one tradition speaks of the various code letters used to designate hidden tithes in its various forms.

This seems to me to be the main purpose of our copper scroll. It is a record of such deposits of sacred material, tithe and tithe vessels, as well as silver and gold and precious vessels, sanctified by dedication or actual use in God's service. The copper scroll and its copy (or copies) were intended to tell the Jewish survivors of the war then raging where this sacred material lay buried, so that if any should be found, it would never be desecrated by profane use. It would also act as a guide to the recovery of the treasure, should it be needed to carry on the war.

The authorship of the scroll will form the subject of Chapter Eighteen, but there remains one question we may suitably deal with here. Why was a comparatively expensive and certainly unusual writing material like copper used for this scroll? It may have been simply a desire to ensure its preservation longer than could be expected of parchment or papyrus. It could also have a ritual significance, since it was decreed that articles made of sheet metal were not susceptible to ritual uncleanness. That would mean that if our scroll became in any way ritually defiled during its interment in the cave, it could, on rediscovery, be washed clean again and fit for priestly handling. One wonders if successive coatings of celluloid solution and aircraft adhesive would be considered to have performed the same function.

CHAPTER SIX

Identification of biblical place names is notoriously uncertain. Towns and villages, well known in their day, have often disappeared without trace. Sometimes their sites have been reused by subsequent generations and renamed. Even when the ancient names have been preserved in more or less recognizable forms, they may nowadays be applied to a village nearby and not to the ancient site itself. The tradition of Christian pilgrims on sacred topography is often helpful, but again not always reliable. Occasionally, place names and their locations can be traced from the ancient records of Mesopotamia or Egypt, or from the Greek historians and geographers. These are valuable, but rarely conclusive. A good modern Bible atlas will give in its identifications the fruit of all these varied sources, weighed and tested by archaeologists and philologists; but few would claim to have arrived at certainty on any but a comparatively small proportion of biblical place names.

Since our scroll sometimes locates its treasure by biblical names we are faced with much the same problems, complicated, moreover, by the fact that our scribe has a habit of using alternatives or synonyms for the more common place names, perhaps with a view to disguising them from the unauthorized reader. Thus, even having resolved our cryptic text to our satisfaction, we are still faced with the difficulty of discovering where first-century tradition located the place. This is not quite the same thing as discovering where the place was in actual fact. The first-century Jew, like the early Christian pilgrim, may quite well have had a strong tradition on the whereabouts of a certain Old Testament site but be just as misled, perhaps by a similarity in the sound of names or even by confusion in the biblical sources themselves. Nevertheless, it is his idea of where it was situated that concerns us in our present search.

The first line of our scroll introduces us to an area very much on the doorstep of Qumran, the Vale of Achor, or "Trouble":

In the fortress which is in the Vale of Achor, forty cubits under the steps entering to the east: a money chest and its contents, of a weight of seventeen talents.

In Joshua 7:24–26, this place is connected with the story of Achan who incurred divine wrath by holding back for his own profit certain of the captured spoil of Jericho, instead of destroying it utterly as religious custom required. The Vale also appears as one of the points on Judah's northeastern frontier (Josh. 15:7), and it is largely from this reference and its context that it can be identified today with fair certainty as the modern *Buqei'a*, or "little plain," a five-mile plateau running above and parallel with the Qumran cliffs (Figures 2–4; Plate 12).

The Vale had an eschatological significance: Hosea speaks of it as the "Gate of Hope" (Hos. 2:15), and Isaiah looks to the day when this part of the wilderness should be a pasture for cattle (Isa. 65:10). This religious importance of the Vale and its surroundings cannot have been lost upon the Essenes at Qumran, for whom the Vale would indeed be the most direct gateway to the new Jerusalem, and for whom it was probably already serving as agricultural land, as it does for the Bedouin today. The Hosea passage might serve as the proof text for the Essene experience of exile and regeneration:

Therefore, behold, I will allure her, and bring her into the wilderness, and speak tenderly to her. And there I will give her vineyards, and make the Vale of Achor a Gate of Hope. And there she shall answer as in the days of her youth, as at the time when she came out of the land of Egypt.

There are a number of ancient fortifications in the area, but "the fortress" can hardly be other than the defense post surmounting a conical hill on the Vale's western edge, ancient Hyrcania, modern *Khirbet* (*el-*) *Mird* (Plate 12). This great castle-fortress was built by the Jewish priest-king John Hyrcanus (135–104 B.C.), who gave it his name.

Soon after John had succeeded to the high priesthood, Judaea entered a period of sixty-six years of independence from foreign domination. The powers of the Seleucid successors of Alexander the Great had gradually been whittled away by family feuds, and from 129 B.C. until the Roman Pompey stormed his way through Palestine, the Jewish state was as free as it had been since the days of the Old Testament kingdom of Judah.

High Priest John took the opportunity of strengthening and enlarging his kingdom, for such had his spiritual principality become. His manner of rule and the military basis of his authority belonged more to a king than a priest. He captured the city of the hated Samaritans in the north, ancient Shechem, and destroyed their temple on Mount Gerizim. To the south he conquered the Edomites and forced them to adopt Jewish religious laws. This extension of his congregation eventually paved the way for the supplanting of his own Hasmonean ruling house, and from that Idumaean clan came the terrible King Herod. In the east, John advanced far beyond the Jordan and nearer home secured his trade routes like the one that ran through the Vale of Achor from Jericho to Bethlehem and beyond.

From the summit of Mird, some eight hundred feet above the plain, the visitor has a wonderful view of the Vale from north to south. Beyond it, to the east lie the misty waters of the Dead Sea, and behind, the purple hills of Moab (Plate 13). Its height and steep sides must have made the fortress virtually impregnable from the east, and on the west the builders had cut it off from the range of hills that lead up to the Jerusalem ridge by a great artificial dry "moat" or ditch. At one place a bridge crosses the ditch and carries an aqueduct that fed the fortress cisterns with water from the hills (Plate 14).

Today the earliest remains visible from the surface are considerably later than the time of John Hyrcanus, for the fortress had a long subsequent use. It served as the refuge of the last of the Maccabean rulers (JA XIII xvi 3; §417) before being destroyed by Gabinius in 57 B.C. The Jewish king, Aristobulos, having tried unsuccessfully to resist Pompey's advance in 63 B.C., had been marched off to Rome as a prisoner, along with his two sons. One of these, Alexander, had escaped and made his way back to Palestine to continue the fight against Roman domination in the person of Gabinius, the Syrian governor. Alexander had taken refuge in the fortress of Alexandrium, whose peak you can still see north of Jericho (Plate 22), and, in an attempt to buy time and safety, delivered up Hyrcania along with Machaerus, on the other side of the Dead Sea (Figure 2; JW I viii 5; §168; JA XIV v 4; §89 f.).

In 56 B.C. Aristobulos had escaped from Rome to continue the resistance (JA XIV vi 1; §92). With him fled his other son, Antigonus (§96), who bided his time. When the Parthians invaded the Roman provinces in the Near East and occupied Syria in 40 B.C., he enlisted their support. He invaded Jerusalem and for three brief years attained his heart's desire of kingship over the Jews. During this time he must have refurbished Hyrcania, for later on, in 31 B.C., his Idumaean supplanter, Herod, captured the fortress from Antigonus' sister (JW I xix 1; §364).

Hyrcania now entered what was probably its grandest phase. Herod seems to have been inordinately proud of his handiwork there when, in 15 B.C., he displayed it to Marcus Agrippa, friend and son-in-law of the emperor, Augustus, on his visit to Palestine (JA XVI ii 1; §13). Hyrcania was now not only a fortress but a palace, one of a chain whose identical construction points to the hand of a common architect.

Like almost everything else connected with that great king, Hyrcania's magnificence was mixed with cruelty and the blood of friend and foe alike. Herod used it as a secret prison to which many of his enemies, suspected of treasonous plotting might be brought and quietly put to death. Characteristically, his own son, Antipater, having been executed in Jericho by his father's dying command, was brought here and buried "without ceremony" (JW I xxxiii 7; §664; JA XVII vii 1; §187).

With all this bloody history behind it, there can be small wonder at the spiritual difficulties encountered four centuries later by a certain St. Saba when he arrived at Hyrcania to spend Lent in A.D. 492, the fifty-third year of his life. The saint had twelve years previously settled in a cave in the Kidron Valley, not far distant, and had later founded there the famous monastery of Mar Saba which today still clings to the precipitous rock face on the side of the gorge.

It is recounted that the saint came to Mird to seek solitude for his religious contemplation. He found the place infested with demons which, despite his anointing the mountain with holy oil, sanctified by being applied to the relics of the True Cross, tormented the saint almost beyond endurance. The evil spirits appeared to him in the form of hideous serpents, ravens, and all kinds of wild beasts. After Easter, Saba returned to Hyrcania, or Kastellion as it was then called in the Greek (a reflection perhaps of the "fortress" of the scroll and certainly of the Syriac *mardā*, "stronghold," from which the modern Arabic name *Mird* is derived), and with his colleagues purified the place thoroughly and erected monastic cells and a church from the building material at hand. This seems to have been in plentiful supply for his chronicler records that they found "a palace, built with marvellously dressed stones and divided into vaulted rooms," doubtless part of the Herodian palace-fortress.

Today the ruins of this monastery, surmounting the conical hill of Khirbet Mird, are plain enough to see. It has been frequently visited but never excavated, for the monks of Mar Saba still retain their rights over it. Indeed, as late as 1925, a group of them set themselves up in its ruins, cleared the church, and constructed for themselves simple cells. They were vexed so much by the attention of the local Bedouin, however, that after several years they had to leave, and the place relapsed once more into ruins.

In 1952 and 1953, the place sprang once more into prominence, for in an underground cavern the Bedouin found scraps of parchment and papyrus texts written in Aramaic, Greek, and Arabic and dating probably from about the eighth–tenth centuries. They ransacked the cave and were later followed by a party of archaeologists from Louvain in Belgium who found more pieces. As well as biblical and classical texts there was a simple letter written in a Christian Aramaic dialect. This has been edited by Father Milik and translated thus:

From Bless-me-my-lord, the sinner Gabriel, to the superior of the Laura of our holy father (Saba).
I beg of you that one may pray for me because of the weariness with which my heart is attainted. Peace be on you from the Father and from the Son and from the Holy Ghost, Amen.

This same weariness of spirit afflicts the visitor even now as he trails up the zigzag path on the western side of the hill. It is not entirely due to its steepness or the heat, for there broods still over Hyrcania some of that atmosphere of grim foreboding and horror that afflicted the good St. Saba and his followers.

In the winter of 1959–60, a party of us visited Mird during an expedition I had arranged to seek out some of the more interesting of the treasure sites of the copper scroll. Our intention was to survey the places for possible future archaeological work, and where possible make small soundings which might, without undue disturbance, throw some light on the topographical features of the treasure inventory. We found that there had been a good deal of vandalism of the surface remains since the last survey in 1953, quite apart from the complete ransacking of the underground chambers that had hidden the documents. At that date the chancel had been furnished with a marble screen, and two marble posts once belonging to it we found thrown down the hillside. The floor of the church is covered with a plain mosaic, but nearby a small room had a beautiful colored mosaic floor of about ten feet square, incorporating the figure of a bird in four colors. Unfortunately this had been largely hacked away, and the whole place was in such disrepair that I asked our archaeological surveyor, G. R. H. ("Mick") Wright, to make a thorough surface survey of the ruin so that it might be permanently recorded before more damage should remove the last traces of ancient construction.

Of course, our main interest was in the Herodian substructure of the Byzantine constructions. It soon became apparent that nothing short of a thorough excavation could reveal the full extent of the palace-fortress. Mick was able, however, to point out one or two stretches of Herodian masonry on the line of probable enclosing walls, with their corner towers. Within the enclosure, the building platform had been leveled up by means of underground vaults, two alone being at present accessible and running parallel north and south. The eastern one is easily reached down modern stairs, but the western, much better preserved, can only be entered by rope or wire ladder from a cistern head. With some trepidation, we fixed our electron ladder around the low stone parapet above the opening, and let each other down into the void, a nylon rope securely tied around our waists and held by the remaining members of the party (Plate 15).

At the bottom, our torches showed that we were in a great vaulted cistern some forty feet long, sixteen feet wide, and twenty-five feet high. The masonry of the roof was beautifully made and fitted without the use of mortar. It was reminiscent of the vaulted cisterns under the old Antonia fortress of the Temple court in Jerusalem (see below, pp. 85 f., Chapter Nine). This also was Herod's work, and standing there in the gloom, we could estimate something of the original grandeur of this desert palace that could evoke the wonder of a Roman prince.

Hard hydraulic plaster covered the floor and sides of the vault indicating that it had certainly been used for the storage of water at some time, but whether this was its original use or not cannot be certain. Mick thought that the Byzantine layout of ranges of rooms around the three sides of the court probably followed the lines of the Herodian structure and cited the example of the mighty fortress of Masada farther south along the shore of the Dead Sea.

Where the original eastern entrance lay, we cannot now tell, and so are unable to define the treasure site "forty cubits under the steps entering to the east." I did wonder, however, whether we might have more success in locating the next item on the scroll, supposing it to be in the vicinity:

In the sepulchral monument, in the third course of stones: 100 bars of gold.

Standing at the present entrance into the court on the western side, you can see some three hundred yards to the southwest a rubble construction crowning the peak of a small promontory overlooking the plain (Figure 5). At first sight it appears to be a lookout post, and from the top you can indeed obtain a wonderful view across the Vale of Achor. But closer inspection shows it to be more monumental in character. The platform which juts out on the northwestern side faces the only way of approach, but is on the opposite side to the open plain. The upper part of the monument has suffered considerable damage at the hands of vandals, but the plan is clear enough. It was laid out as a square of some thirty-three feet around a pinnacle of rock, the substantial retaining walls being skillfully keyed into the irregular rock surface and made to appear to grow out of the natural slope of the hill (Plate 16). The space thus enclosed about the pinnacle was then filled in with rubble. Pottery embedded in the cracks between the boulders of the retaining walls showed clearly that the monument was another relic of Herodian times.

Mick Wright thought that it could well have been a funerary monument, and certainly there was no difficulty in determining the "third course of stones." We had with us metal and cavity detectors of the most advanced type, together with a scientist from England to operate them, but we discovered that the rock of the hillside had a natural magnetism that made it very difficult to differentiate a "natural" response in the instruments to one caused by the presence of metal. Needless to say, there was no thought of destroying the whole monument on the off-chance that it might be the treasure cache of the copper scroll.

Quite apart from the inventory, this funerary monument, if such it be, is most intriguing. We know that Herod executed a number of his most important prisoners here, and we actually found a group of Herodian graves lying out on a low hillside to the east of Mird (Figure 5). But none of these was so distinguished-looking as to warrant the provision of such a monument alongside the palace-fortress. I could not help wondering whether we might not be within a stone's throw of a really important tomb, and if so, to whom it could have belonged.

Josephus tells us that Herod himself died in Jericho, dropsical, gangrenous, and tortured with burning pains. He

was borne upon a golden bier studded with precious stones of various kinds and with a cover of purple over it. The dead man too was wrapped in purple robes and wore a diadem on which a gold crown had been placed, and beside his right hand lay a sceptre. Round the bier were his sons and a host of relatives, and after them came the army disposed according to the various nationalities and designations. They were arranged in the following order: first came his bodyguards, then the Thracians, and following them whatever Germans he had, and next came the Gauls. These men were all equipped for battle. Right behind them came the whole army as if marching to war, led by their company-commanders and lower officers, and they were followed by five hundred servants carrying spices (JA XVII viii 3; §196 f.).

Fragrant spices they would certainly need if, as the following description of their funeral journey seems to imply, they were to make a stately progress of a mile a day for twenty-five days "towards Herodium" near Bethlehem, in the heat of early summer. In fact the account in *Antiquities* merely states the procession advanced a mile "towards Herodium," while the parallel account in *Wars* (I xxxiii 9; §673) says the body was carried "two hundred stades to Herodium." This place is usually assumed to be the palace-fortress surmounting the conical hill some eight miles south of Bethlehem (Figure 2), and this was certainly meant by the writer or redactor of *Wars*. But I have often thought that it would have been considerably more comfortable, not to say hygienic, for the retinue if they had progressed through the Vale of Achor no farther than this other palace-fortress of Hyrcania at the foot of the Judaean hills. We know it by the name of its first architect, but it hardly seems likely that Herod and his followers would have continued to give their new creation the name of the Maccabean ruler of a century before. Perhaps therefore, there has been some confusion and that it was to Khirbet Mird that the long and splendid funerary procession wended its way, and that somewhere here there still remains to be discovered the fabulously rich tomb of the Idumaean king.

Another mystery tantalized our little expedition during its visit to Mird. To the north of the fortress, the hill falls steeply to a narrow wadi, at one point no more than two or three yards wide. Here, cut into the cliff on the south side of the wadi, we found the entrance to a tunnel which ran down in a series of steps at an angle of about thirty degrees, a hundred feet or so into the solid rock (Figure 5; Plate 17). It may well go on even farther, but some busy hands had laboriously cleared out the dust and rubble this far and then apparently given up. A little along the wadi bed was another tunnel, but only the first step or two of this one had been cleared.

The purpose of these shafts, wide enough for a man and with sufficient headroom to stand upright, is a mystery. The entrance is about six feet above the present wadi bed in the one case, but the more obstructed shaft is very little above the level of the watercourse. Another such tunnel about six miles to the north has been known for a long time. It is cut into the cliff on the north side of the Jerusalem-Jericho road just before it debouches into the Jordan valley. Here again, it has only been partly excavated and nobody seems to know its purpose. One thing only is certain: to cut such tunnels must have been a most laborious task and would not have been attempted for fun. Even at the depth so far penetrated the air is heavy and warm and to clear away the rubbish would need the provision of some form of forced air supply and a regular and frequent change of workers at the face. Short of a complete excavation it is impossible to tell at what period the tunnels were made, but it is difficult to disassociate those at Mird from the fortress towering above.

It seems very probable, too, that there was a connection between the activities of Herod's fortress and the fortunes of the Essene settlement at Qumran, barely six miles away to the east. The archaeologists tell us that the monastery remained uninhabited for most of King Herod's reign. This is perhaps not surprising in view of Herod's decree forbidding all public and private concourse (JA XV x 4; §365 f.), and the proximity of his secret prison. Later on, in the sixth century, there existed a very real link between Mird and the Essene establishment at Qumran. To the south of the monastery is a spring called 'Ain Feshkha (Figure 4; PDSS Plates 117–21). The people of the Scrolls had used this freshwater spring quite extensively for plantations, as recent archaeological work has shown. So also did the hermits of the Mount of Kastellion who, we are told in one ancient chronicle, possessed "a garden six miles distant, near the sea shore, almost on the bank." The archaeologists found at 'Ain Feshkha the remains of a small house of the Byzantine period, presumably that of the establishment's resident gardener to whom the chronicler actually refers. In the vicinity of the spring dwelt also a hermit shepherd named Sophronios who lived there

61

for seventy years in a cave, stark naked. Even demons, we are told, kept at a respectful distance of three furlongs from his dwelling.

The Qumran area seems to me to be the reference of a whole group of items of our copper scroll inventory, and its inclusion raises a number of interesting questions.

CHAPTER SEVEN

"In the wilderness, Beth-arabah, Middin, Secacah, Nibshan, the City of Salt, and En-gedi: six cities with their villages" (Josh. 15:61–62).

Thus the Book of Joshua lists the desert settlements of Judah, from Beth-arabah, modern *'Ain Gharabah*, southwest of Jericho, to the spring of En-gedi, modern *'Ain Jidi*, halfway down the western shore of the Dead Sea (Figure 2). Between these two extremes lay four "cities" which have never been certainly identified. One of them, Secacah, appears a number of times in our scroll:

21. In the dam (?) that is in the Valley of Secacah, buried at one cubit: 12 talents of silver.

22. At the head of the water conduit [which penetrates (?)] Secacah from the north, buried th[ree] cubits under the great [. . .]: 7 talents of silver.

23. In the fissure that is in Secacah, in the spo[ut(?)] of the "Solomon" reservoir: tithe vessels arranged side by side (?).

24. Sixty cubits from the "Solomon" aqueduct toward the great watchtower, buried at three cubits: 23 talents of silver.

25. In the tomb which is in the Wadi *Kippā'*, on the way from Jericho to Secacah, buried at seven cubits: 32 talents.

There is nothing in the Bible to indicate where in this twenty-six-mile stretch of wilderness bordering the Dead Sea Secacah might be, except that it lay presumably to the north of the area, since only Middin stood between it and Beth-arabah. Furthermore, since the most habitable stretch of country between Beth-arabah and En-gedi is the Vale of Achor, we may reasonably locate at least Middin and Secacah, the most northerly of the "cities of the wilderness," in that area. This finds support in our scroll's references to the Vale, and the further clues it offers concerning Secacah help us locate that "city" with fair certainty.

The term used in Item 21 for the "Valley" of Secacah (*gê*) denotes a narrower opening than Achor's "Vale" (*'ēmeq*). A *gê*, which can often be rendered "gorge" or "ravine," can, in fact, cut across an *'ēmeq*. We may deduce, therefore, that Secacah lay near such a ravine, to which it gave its name. Item 25 tells us that the route from Jericho to Secacah ran by or across a wadi called *Kippā'*, otherwise quite unknown, which was presumably near to Secacah, and thus associated with its "gorge." It seems to me that the only place which at all fits the topographical situation envisaged by our scroll is Khirbet Qumran itself. It stands by a "gorge," alongside a "wadi," across which ran an ancient route from Jericho (Figure 3). The site of Qumran we know from archaeological excavations has a history extending back into Old Testament times and has long been identified with one or other of the "cities of the wilderness." It has, furthermore, a "watchtower," a water "aqueduct," a "conduit," and a very noticeable earthquake "fissure" which runs right through a large "reservoir" (Figure 6; Plate 18).

It seems very probable that we can actually date the earthquake that caused such havoc in the little monastery. At that time many of the walls collapsed and there seems to have been a fire which ravaged the buildings and left a layer of cinders from the blazing roof timbers and reeds scattered over the open courtyards. Josephus records an earthquake which occurred in the seventh year of King Herod's reign, in the spring of 31 B.C., not long before the Battle of Actium was to decide the fate of the civilized world. He says that the earthquake was unprecedented in severity, killing many cattle and about thirty thousand people in the ruins of their houses. Herod's army, however, was encamped in the plains of Jericho and were thus physically unharmed though terrified by what seemed to them a most unhappy omen of the outcome of their impending battle with the Arabs (JW I xix 3; §370; JA XV v 2; §121 f.).

In Qumran, the great cistern on the east side of the settlement was split down its length, so that one side dropped some two feet lower than the other. The hard hydraulic plaster remained in position on either side of the crack, although in places the soil underneath had dropped away, leaving a gap between it and the underside of the plaster "shell" which would have served well as a deposit for treasure. During our expedition we were able to crawl inside this compartment, and found there a few pieces of broken pottery. Little more could be hoped from such an obvious hiding place, for when the Jews were driven from Qumran in A.D. 68 the Roman soldiers moved in to convert it into a small military outpost guarding the way from Jericho, just as the ancient Israelites had done seven or eight centuries before. Doubtless they would have spent their spare time searching the ruins for any trophies or valuables their enemies might have left, and the gaping earthquake fissure would not have gone unnoticed.

All the same, there was one treasure in Qumran the Romans did miss. In a room on the west side of the monastery (*PDSS* Plate 173), the archaeologists discovered three little juglets buried under the floor, packed with over five hundred silver coins (Plate 19). They consisted of tetradrachmae that had been minted in Tyre at various times in the first century B.C. Who put them there, and whether they could conceivably be connected with our treasure scroll nobody knows for certain. Naturally those who like to think the copper scroll is a fairy tale deny any possible connection. One such protagonist has offered the suggestion that some thief from Jericho came to Qumran one day when the monks were not in residence and hid his ill-gotten gains under the floor of one of their rooms. When later he came to collect his hoard he found to his dismay that the Essenes were again at home and had to slink away and leave the treasure for twentieth-century archaeologists.

An aqueduct brought rainwater into the monastery from a dam set in the cliffs behind. During a few weeks of the year it would rain heavily enough on the foothills of the Judaean wilderness for the water to flow into the wadis and be carried across the Vale to the edge of the cliffs. There it would tumble onto the plateau beneath or, in the case of the Wadi Qumran, fall into a gorge and be carried alongside the monastery down to the sea. The Essenes had constructed a simple barrage to capture a flow from the waterfall and lead it along a plastered conduit, through a tunnel hewn out of the solid rock, and thence by way of another conduit along the cliff face to the head of the aqueduct and down the plateau to the monastery. There it was

PLATE 1. The unopened rolls of copper.

PLATE 2. Henri de Contenson.

PLATE 3. A roll mounted on its spindle preparatory to cutting.

PLATE 4. Professor H. Wright Baker cutting a segment of the scroll.

PLATE 5. A newly cut segment.

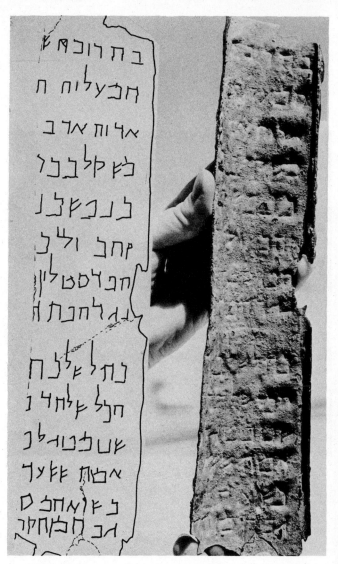

PLATE 6. A segment showing part of the first column of the engraving together with a facsimile of the text.

PLATE 7. Dr. Awni Dajani, Director of Antiquities, Jordan, with Professor Karl Georg Kuhn.

PLATE 8. The Wadi Qumran, the ruins of the Essene monastery, and the Dead Sea.

PLATE 9. Cleaning a segment of the scroll with a dental brush.

PLATE 10. The completely open scroll.

PLATE 11. Father Joseph T. Milik.

PLATE 12. The Vale of Achor *(Buqei'a)* and, on the right, Hyrcania *(Khirbet el-Mird)*.

PLATE 13. Mird from the west.

PLATE 14. The Herodian aqueduct at the foot of Mird.

PLATE 15. Inside a Mird cistern.

PLATE 16. The monument at Mird.

PLATE 17. Inside the stepped tunnel at Mird.

led past a simple breakwater into a large settling tank and thence through a series of channels and conduits to fill seven large cisterns scattered about the monastery. All these installations—dam, rock-hewn conduit, aqueduct, and cisterns—are there today, wonderfully preserved, and corresponding remarkably with the details of the copper scroll (*PDSS* Plates 142–158).

Why the reservoir and aqueduct should be called by the name of Solomon is uncertain. It may have been simply that in the first century, at the time when our scroll was written, they were already considered ancient and, as so often with antiquities, were arbitrarily linked with the name of a great hero of the past. I think it more probable, however, that such water installations as these were typified as "Solomonic" because of some tradition that this great builder and innovator was responsible for the construction and distribution of their prototypes in the "Golden Age." The famous "Pools of Solomon," south of Bethlehem, which in fact go back no earlier than the second century B.C., may owe their name to the same typification.

During our short expedition we brought instruments to bear on the floors and walls of the monastery, without, however, much hope of detecting metals. Not only were we again troubled with the magnetic rocks abounding in the construction, but the stated depths of deposits were far out of the range of our instruments, which were designed to detect metals and cavities at hardly more than eighteen inches. We decided it was worth while making one very shallow trench outside the main group of buildings, in an open courtyard which seemed to be at a point indicated by the scroll. Again, where our instruments detected a strong reaction at the western end of the Hall of Congregation (Plate 20), as the largest room of the settlement has been called, our narrow trench brought to light an oven and a group of broken pottery completely overlooked by former archaeologists.

One of the puzzles of the copper scroll lies in just what kind of substances are implied in the word "tithes" mentioned so often. Milik wants to translate this word everywhere as "essence" or the like, and philologically this is quite possible. But in post-biblical Jewish literature it came to mean anything set aside for sacred purposes, and I think we should give it this wider meaning in our scroll, as I have already described in Chapter Five. It will have been noticed that the treasure deposit in the earthquake fissure of Secacah consisted of "tithe vessels," which makes our finding of broken pieces of pots under the plaster of some interest, though by no means conclusive evidence that we had hit upon the very spot.

Tithe could consist of agricultural produce and cattle products, and among the archaeological puzzles of Qumran there have been discoveries which might possibly have some bearing on this feature of our scroll. Concealed underground in various places within and without the monastery buildings were found some scores of cooking pots, mostly broken, but all containing the bones of animals that had apparently been eaten in some form of ritual meals (*PDSS* Plates 125, 126). It is some measure of our ignorance of the religious practices of the Jews of this time that the precise nature of these feasts cannot be determined, but we can hazard the guess at least that the deposits were made in order that neither the vessels nor their contents should be used for any non-sacred purpose, like the treasure of our copper scroll. Our short expedition was able, incidentally, to add one more to this collection of sacred meals deposits. It was found, not underground as with the others, but hidden inside an interior wall of one of the rooms, close by the treasure deposits of silver coins. Again, it was one of our scientific instruments that detected the presence of this pottery. One wonders how much else of importance previous archaeologists have missed for want of the means of detecting underground features so abundantly offered by modern scientific research.

To reach Qumran today, the visitor will normally come by car along a tarmac road from Jerusalem, Jericho, or Amman to the head of the Dead Sea. Then at the police post he will turn off onto a dirt track that follows the shoreline for about four miles and then turns sharply inward toward the monastery plateau at the foot of the cliffs, about two miles from the coast. The latter part of this route follows an ancient track that could well be the "way from Jericho to Secacah" of our scroll (Figure 3). It is certainly on this side that we find the cemeteries of Qumran. The largest extends immediately eastward of the settlement buildings to the edge of the plateau, and contains about eleven hundred graves, neatly arranged north-south (*PDSS* Plates 176, 177). The bodies were laid in a niche on the eastward side of the trench, about four-and-a-half feet down, and, as one might expect in such a community dedicated to voluntary poverty, little or no tomb furniture was found with the bodies.

Other burials were also found to the north, south, and east of the main cemetery, but the graves were not so neatly orientated, and the burials here included women and children (*PDSS* Plate 178). No tomb has appeared as yet actually in the side of the wadi to my knowledge, although I have seen some more ancient burials dug into the soft limestone sides of a watercourse a little way to the north.

It may be that the route from Jericho referred to was another which can be easily traced today, though not amenable to motor traffic at its Qumran end. This runs closely by the foot of the cliffs and so enters the monastery from the northwest. Undoubtedly the wadis in the immediate vicinity of Qumran, and particularly where they are crossed by these two ancient routes, merit a very close inspection.

CHAPTER EIGHT

Item 58 would seem, at first sight, to bear an unmistakable location:

> In Mount Gerizim, under the ascent of its upper ditch: one chest and its contents, and 60 talents of silver.

The biblical Mount Gerizim stands above ancient Shechem, near modern Nablus, some thirty miles north of Jerusalem (Figure 1; *PDSS* 92, 93). With its companion mount, Ebal, it dominates the plain and the two important passes to the west and north. At its foot runs the ancient road to Jerusalem, skirting the well where Jesus spoke with the Samaritan woman (John 4:5 f.). For Mount Gerizim was, and is, the religious center of the Samaritan sect and, from the fourth to the second century B.C., was the site of their Temple, rival to the Jewish sanctuary at Jerusalem.

While there is no doubt at all about the location of this Mount Gerizim, there must be considerable misgivings about the correctness of such an identification for the treasure repository of our scroll. In the first place, the directions given, "under the ascent of its upper ditch," are too vague to locate adequately a hiding place on several acres of hilltop dotted with dozens of pits and cisterns. Second, the hiding of Jewish sacred treasure in a Samaritan holy place is inconceivable. These considerations alone should prompt us to seek a pseudonym in our "Mount Gerizim," and preferably a place nearer Qumran or Jerusalem.

There was, in fact, another "Mount Gerizim," for Jewish tradition going back at least to the first Christian centuries maintained that the true site of Gerizim and Ebal was not in Samaritan territory at all, but near Jericho. The grounds for this anti-Samaritan (and historically quite erroneous) contention were found in Deuteronomy 11:29–30, where the mountains are apparently linked topographically with Gilgal, which certainly lay near Jericho. A certain Rabbi Eleazar of the second century A.D. affirmed that the biblical text referred not to the mountains above Shechem but to two artificial mounds called by the same names and erected by the Israelites themselves. This idea took strong root in early Christian circles, and the famous sixth-century mosaic map at Madeba in Transjordan shows Gerizim and Ebal above Elisha's fountain in ancient Jericho.

Unfortunately, no other ancient authority gives us sufficient information to identify southern "Gerizim" and "Ebal" with certainty. A number of suggestions have been made by scholars, however, and one seems particularly well conceived. Behind Jericho, where the great gorge of the Wadi Kelt debouches onto the open plain, stand two high mounds, in their final form certainly artificial constructions (Figure 7). They rise on either side of the old Jericho-Jerusalem road and in their position and general aspect are not unlike the true Gerizim and Ebal of the north, although, of course, much smaller (Plate 21). At the foot of the southern hill is a village known by the name of Jabr (dialectically *gabr*), which is perhaps a recollection of the name Cypros given to the hill itself by Herod the Great after his mother. For it seems very probable

72

that the fortified mounds which the first-century Jews of Jericho fastened upon as being the biblical Gerizim and Ebal were, in fact, the creations of King Herod, part of a series of military posts defending the eastern approaches to Jerusalem.

One of these, Hyrcania, we have already discussed at length, but it is worth looking at the whole of this defense system since it gives us a clue to the proper understanding of our scroll. Taking the west bank of the Jordan River first, we have the northernmost fortress above the mouth of the Wadi Far'ah to the east of modern Nablus. It crowns the top of Mount Sartaba and derived its name Alexandrium from its reputed founder, Alexander Jannaeus (Plate 22). Fifteen miles to the south is the Maccabean fortress of Docus (Figure 18), and this has particular interest for us since it appears to be the site of the treasure deposits of Item 32. Then we have our pseudo-Gerizim, Cypros, with its companion fortress, Taurus, dominating the Jericho-Jerusalem road and Herod's New Jericho, and eleven miles to the south, Hyrcania, modern Khirbet Mird. Herodium lay four miles to the southeast of Bethlehem, and again overlooking the Dead Sea (Figure 2), the grandest creation of all, Masada, twenty-five miles southeast.

On the east of the sea there was the infamous Machaerus where Josephus tells us Salome danced and John the Baptist was beheaded, some eight miles north of the gorge of the biblical Arnon (Figure 2). Josephus speaks of another Herodium in this area, probably to be located below Mount Nebo, near the northeastern shore of the sea.

The nine fortresses formed a closely integrated system, the creation of a master planner. For a description of their construction and function I cannot do better than quote my friend, Stewart Perowne, with whom I had the pleasure of first visiting some of these sites a few years ago.

They have certain features in common which stamp them as being recognizably the work of a single school of military architecture, as are the fortresses of Vauban and his imitators. First, they are all on the tops of hills or mountains. Second, the stone building on the summit is, wherever possible, protected by a glacis so steep that it is barely possible to walk straight up it. Third, in the base of the final cone, at the foot of the glacis, are vast cisterns, one or more, excavated in the hill, and lined with hydraulic cement, to store rain water. Taurus, with a perennial aqueduct at its base, had only one: Alexandrium, twelve. Fourth, wherever possible an aqueduct has brought additional supplies of water, generally rain catchment from adjacent hills or *wadis*, but in the case of the great Herodium from springs, to be stored in a large open tank, thus reserving the inner cisterns for use in emergency and siege. Fifth, the actual cone of the fort is severed from the *massif* from which it protrudes by an artificial fosse.

These five features are the marks of the "Herodian" fortress, and nearly all of them are found in all nine of which the sites are now known and accessible. Below Herodium, Alexandrium and Machaerus, faubourgs, of which traces remain, were attached to the actual forts, because they were dwelling-places, as well as citadels.

Every castle in the system could signal at least to one another, in most cases to more than one. Herodium, Machaerus, Docus and Cypros could signal direct to Jerusalem as well. Where a fort was not visible from its neighbour (as in the case of Alexandrium and Cypros, 16 miles to the south), detached signal-stations were constructed on the nearest vantage-point. Sometimes, as at Machaerus, a relay-station was necessary to surmount an intervening hill. The exact method of signalling is unknown to us. In the air of Palestine visibility is good. It is possible, for instance, on some days in winter, when the atmosphere has been washed by rain, to see the snowcap of Mount Hermon from the north end of the Dead Sea, 100 miles away. That fire signals were used at night by the Nabateans we know from Diodorus Siculus (XIX, 97), and by the Jews, from the Mishnah (Rosh ha-Shana 24) which mentions Sartaba (Alexandrium) as one of the stations.[1]

None of these fortresses has been fully excavated. Standing on the upper slopes of Cypros ("Gerizim"), one can see plainly the outline of the fortress on a protruding shoulder, with an adjoining tower marked by fallen stones (Plate 23). Just inside the tower is the open mouth of a cistern. While there, our expedition tried clearing this shaft, but after some twenty feet found that it was only then beginning to bell out and could well have extended a further fifty feet below (Plate 24). Where the "upper ditch" or "pit" of the scroll might be, only a full excavation of the fortress' main features and defense works could tell.

The fortress of Docus had a particularly bloody history. In February, of the year 135 B.C., Simon the Maccabee and his two sons, Mattathias and Judas, were treacherously killed in Docus by his son-in-law, Ptolemy. Simon had been visiting the country provinces to see that they were being well governed and was received at Jericho by Ptolemy, the son of Abubus, who had been appointed chief of the district. But as the First Book of the Maccabees says, "his heart was lifted up and he determined to make himself master of the country. . . . And the son of Abubus treacherously welcomed them into the fortress called Dok which he had built, and prepared a great feast for

[1] Stewart Perowne, *The Life and Times of Herod the Great*, London: Hodder and Stoughton, 1956, pp. 106 f.

them. But he hid men there. When Simon and his sons were drunk, Ptolemy and those with him stood up, took their weapons, and came into the banqueting hall after Simon, and cut him down with his two sons and certain of his young slaves . . ." (I Macc. 16:11–16).

When Ptolemy's bid for power failed, he was forced to take refuge in the fortress of Docus and was attacked there by Simon's third son, John, who had now assumed his father's high-priestly office. Unfortunately, Ptolemy had managed to capture John's mother and remaining brothers as hostages. He hauled them onto the wall and tortured them in full view of his attackers and threatened to hurl them down headlong if John did not give up the siege. For a time John held back, but his mother, so Josephus tells us, "stretched out her hands, beseeching him not to weaken on her account, but to give way to his anger so much the more, and make every effort to take the place and get his foe into his power and avenge those dearest to him. For, she said, it would be pleasant for her to die in torment if the enemy, who was doing these things to them, paid the penalty for his crimes against them."

John thereupon pressed on with the siege, but operations were halted by the onset of the sabbath year, during which the Jews remained inactive as they did on the sabbath day. Ptolemy took advantage of the observance by escaping over the Jordan to Amman, having first killed his hostages (JA XIII viii 1; §230 f.).

At least as early as the time of the Crusaders, Mount Docus was identified with the site of Christ's temptation in the wilderness, and a hermitage had been built there since A.D. 340 (Plate 25). Its association with the forty days of fasting earned it the name of *Quarantana,* and in medieval times there was a zigzag path up the steep side of the mountain to a chapel dedicated to Mary and an altar in the form of a cross. Nearby, halfway up the mountain, was the traditional site where Jesus sat. On the peak itself, near one of the Crusader citadels, the place where the devil reposed was also shown to the energetic pilgrim. The view from the top, from Hermon in the north to the Moabite frontier in the south, over the Jordan plain and the Dead Sea, and westward to the Judaean highlands, was and is certainly extensive. It was a wonderful fortress site, and hardly to be missed in the Herodian defense system. Again, only a full excavation could indicate where the "eastern corner of the guardhouse" of Item 32, might have lain, and how the treasure deposit of twenty-two talents might have been reached, some ten-and-a-half feet beneath the surface.

Today, the spring of 'Ain Dūk at the foot of the Mount of Temptation recalls the ancient name. In the lower slopes recently excavated caves have produced skeletons and other remains that may well have come from the time of Simon and promise that a thorough search of the area would be well worth while.

Whoever put the treasure of our scroll into its hiding places must obviously have been in possession of the sites named. At the very beginning of the second Jewish Revolt the rebels wisely seized Cypros from its Roman garrison (JW II viii 6; §484 f.), and only gave it up when Vespasian reached Jericho in June 68 (JW IV viii 1; §450). It seems reasonable to assume that they would have secured command of the other fortresses in the vicinity to control Jerusalem's eastern approaches. We seem to have, then, a clue to the authorship of our scroll, and this receives added weight when we come to examine those treasure caches in the Holy City itself.

CHAPTER NINE

It is in and around Jerusalem that the greater part of the scroll's treasure was deposited. Quite apart from its main purpose, the ability of our text to throw light on the topography of the city in the first century A.D. must rank it high among contemporary sources. Written in the language of the period and the place, it can here and there serve as a welcome corrective to the Greek of Josephus and the New Testament, hitherto our main literary sources of information. For the rest we have relied upon the Old Testament for our knowledge of the city's growth and development and on rabbinic tradition for information mainly on the Temple and its services. Archaeological investigation really begins with the work of the American scholar Edward Robinson in the early nineteenth century, although we have eye-witness accounts of the Byzantine city from Christian pilgrims of the fourth century onward.

It was in 1864 that the first great attempt to map subterranean Jerusalem was begun, under the leadership of a handful of British Army officers and men working under the most hazardous conditions with very little financial or moral support. Nothing like this survey has ever again been possible, and the world stands in a tremendous debt of gratitude to those men for their courage in attempting such a work and for

79

the meticulous care with which they published their findings.

Great projects often have small and comparatively trivial beginnings. For some time the British press had been carrying stories of the scandal perpetuated in the Holy City by an insufficient or nonexistent sanitary system. The accumulated rubbish of the centuries puckered the noses of Victorian gentility in faraway England to such an extent that a fund was raised toward making a plan of the underground city, preparatory to reorganizing its water supplies. Armed with the princely sum of five hundred pounds (about $1,400 at the present rate of exchange) the gift of a certain Miss Burdett Coutts, the Palestine Exploration Fund approached the British Army for help, and before long a party of Royal Engineers, under the command of Captain (later Sir) Charles Wilson, sailed for the Holy Land (the gallant officer bearing his own expenses). Afterward, Captain (later Sir) Charles Warren followed to carry on the work, supported by his trusty aide, Corporal (later Sergeant) Birtles. We shall have many occasions in the pages that follow to refer to the work of these men and here and there to quote verbatim from their records. Their technical reports are models of painstaking accuracy, and their more popular works contain much that is entertaining and exciting, with occasional glimpses into the gravity of the risks they took in their enterprise. Warren's main object was nothing less than the methodical exploration of the Muslim sanctuary itself, to lay bare the tantalizing secrets of its underground passageways and caverns, long hidden from the sight of infidels and indeed, most of the Faithful.

Warren did not do all that he wanted by any means;

the suspicion and chicanery of the resident Turkish authorities, coupled with obscurantism and downright stupidity on the part of certain of his committee at home, put such physical, political, and financial barriers in his way as would have deterred a lesser man from the very beginning. He was obliged to confine his investigations almost completely to the outer walls of the Muslim sanctuary, usually by sinking deep shafts and driving tunnels from them to the walls and foundations he wished to examine. With the equipment at his disposal, and harried continually on all sides, this was a most dangerous procedure and archaeologically of very limited value. These were the days before dating by pottery types, when much had still to be learned about stratification and ancient building construction; these pioneer explorers were often throwing away as rubbish the kind of material which, a century later, would have told a story on its own account and put the remainder of their work on a more secure chronological basis.

Since those days a succession of archaeological excavations have been launched in and around Jerusalem, but never on the same immense scale and rarely within the walled city. Great and detailed as the work has been, there is no doubt that should even such limited opportunities as were made available to Wilson and Warren recur, many more of the problems which beset historical research into this most exciting of cities could be solved. In such work our copper scroll will henceforth have a major part to play.

There is probably no archaeological site in Palestine that offers so much promise and yet so many difficulties in excavation as Jerusalem. Not only has it suffered repeated destruction and rebuilding over the course of some three thousand years but the present density of population within the walled city makes normal surface exploration virtually impossible. Even the natural contours of the city area have changed, as man has leveled the hills for defensive or sacred purposes and over the centuries filled the valleys with his rubbish.

The city area lay across two rocky spurs, lower than the surrounding summits but cut off from them on three sides by abrupt ravines (Figure 8). Thus, on the west, south, and east sides the city had natural defenses, formed by the lines of the Hinnom and Kidron valleys. To the north, however, Jerusalem lay comparatively unprotected, and it was always from that direction that her enemies made their attacks. In consequence, it was here that the city's rulers paid special attention to her artificial defenses, which required modification and addition as the city spread out to the north, the only direction of growth possible.

A third major valley, now hardly discernible, divided the city in two, running obliquely from the northwest to the southeast and joining the Hinnom Valley just short of its junction with the Kidron. Until now the Hebrew name of that central valley has never been known, for apparently it appeared nowhere in the Old Testament. Thanks to our scroll we now know it to have been called the "Outer Valley" (see below, pp. 89 f.), and the strange name by which Josephus knows it, the "Valley of the Cheesemakers" (thus "Tyropoeon" Valley), to have been a misunderstanding of the original Hebrew word.

About halfway down the length of this Outer Valley (it ran "outside" the old Jebusite city on the southeastern hill), it was joined by another depression, run-

82

ning more or less at right angles to it and dividing the western ridge in two. For want of the original name, this is usually called the "Cross Valley."

Another depression, smaller, but again of some topographical importance, runs down from the northeastern corner of the city and curves eastward to join the Kidron about a hundred yards to the south of St. Stephen's Gate. It is usually called St. Anne's Valley, since it skirts the Basilica of St. Anne, north of the present Muslim sacred area known as the Haram.

These natural divisions cut the city area into four parcels of high ground, the largest of which was the southwesterly. From at least the first century it was this area which was identified with ancient Zion. In fact, all the archaeological and literary evidence points quite conclusively to the southern part of the *eastern* ridge as having been the site of the old Jebusite and later Davidic city. Equally certain is the fact that the area to the north of this, now occupied by the raised and leveled platform of the Haram, was the old Temple area. It was here that Solomon, Zerubbabel, and Herod the Great built their successive temples, and it is in this area that our researches will take us more than in any other.

North of the Temple hill, and divided from it by a small but sharp depression, rose more high ground, the site of the city quarter Josephus calls *Bezetha,* or New City. Some scholars believe that it is this term which lies behind the name given in the New Testament to a pool with five porticoes where the palsied man lay waiting to be put into the waters when they were disturbed (John 5:2). The texts variously read the name of the pool as *Bethzatha, Bethsaida,* and *Bethesda,* but it may well be that Item 56 of our scroll gives at last the contemporary Hebrew underlying the name:

In the House of the Twin Pools (*Beth Eshdathayin,* Bethesda [?]), in the pool as you approach its settling basins: vessels of tithe of [. . .] and tithe of [. . .], arranged side by side (?).

In the New Testament Greek we have the latter part of the name Bethesda in its singular form, in the Hebrew of the scroll it is in the dual, "two slopes." The root seems to imply a place where water pours down or out and the location of the five porticoed pool in the depression just to the north of the Temple area suits this description quite well.

The Gospel story locates the pool near the "sheep-gate," which confirms the northerly direction of the site since Nehemiah's description of this gate requires it to be in the north wall (Neh. 3:1, 32; 12:39).

Already by the fourth century a church had been built over the pool, and today, in the grounds of the lovely Crusader church of St. Anne the visitor can see the authentic remains of the double pool of Bethesda. Recent excavations are bringing even more of this very fine group of buildings to light (Plate 26).

The word I have rendered "settling basins" is probably a diminutive of the normal word for "large basin" and does, I think, offer a solution to a most intriguing problem connected with the nearby fortress of Antonia.

Herod built this great stronghold at the northwestern corner of the Temple area, overlooking the artificial moat that continued the natural depression which separated the northeastern hill from the sanctuary (Figure 8). He named the fortress after his friend and patron, Anthony, the Roman conqueror of Syria and Palestine (JA XV xi 4; §409), a kindly thought which did little to enhance Herod's popularity with his Jewish subjects. The high-priestly vestments were kept in its chambers, making even the functioning of the Temple services dependent on the good will of the Roman garrison usually stationed there.

The Antonia fortress played an important part in the defense and eventual destruction of the city and its Temple. Describing this last, bitter campaign, Josephus says that the Roman legions threw up an embankment "over against the middle of the pool called Strouthion" (JW V xi 4; §467). The only pool in this area which at all suits the context is the great double cistern lying obliquely north-northwest–south-southeast under the fortress itself (Figure 9). Today the remains of the Antonia fortress lie under the Convent of the Sisters of Zion who will show the visitor excavated remains of Herod's stronghold, including part of the old pavement which many identify with "The Pavement" on which Pilate sat in judgment on Jesus (John 19:13). With the permission of the Convent's Superior, you may be led below the kitchens to the great double cistern, the wonderfully constructed vaulting of which is so characteristically "Herodian" (see above, p. 57, Plate 27). This again is one of the few parts of Jerusalem bearing authentic witness to the city of Jesus' time, but if this is the pool referred to by Josephus in connection with his account of the Roman attack on the Temple area, it poses two problems. First, there is the strange Greek name he gives the double cistern, and second, the equally strange manner of describing the position of the Roman embankment by reference to an underground reservoir in the very heart of the fortress itself.

To take the name first: the Greek diminutive *strou-*

thion means "any small bird, especially of the sparrow kind." Yet "sparrow" seems hardly a fitting name for this great double cistern whose tanks measure 165 and 127 feet in length and some 20 feet in width, and no satisfactory explanation of the name has yet been forthcoming. As elsewhere it seems likely that the Greek redactors have misinterpreted the historian's original Semitic.

The clue, I think, lies in the word I have rendered "settling basins" in Item 56, *y^emimah*, which is exactly the same as the name of Job's daughter, Jemimah (Job 42:14), and is the name of a bird, usually of the pigeon type, in Hebrew and kindred dialects. It seems that those ancient scholars were confused by the similarity and misread the technical term for settling basin as the name of a small bird, supposing it to have been the name of the pool instead of part of it. It is as if someone not overfamiliar with Semitic syntax read the original as if the technical term were the name "Jemima" given to the pool as Herod gave the names of his womenfolk to towers and fortresses.

On this supposition, what Josephus wanted to say was not that the Romans built their rampart "over against the middle of the pool called Strouthion," but "over against the middle of the settling basin(s) of the pool."

The topographical situation now becomes clear. Examination has shown that the double cistern was fed from an aqueduct running from the north, and the Survey officers speak of a long conduit leading down from outside the Damascus Gate. All that apparently remains of that channel is a long section at the southern end, cut into the rock beneath the pavement of the street called *Sheikh Rihān*. At the junction of this street with *'Aqabet el-Hindiyeh*, the canal runs to the double cistern through two slightly divergent branches, which distribute their waters into a number of small settling basins. The water is there decanted and flows on to penetrate into the double cistern through openings arranged on the summit of the vaults. Originally, it may have entered directly into the northern end of the western tank, where there is a small, irregularly shaped chamber (Plate 28), probably intended to serve as a large basin.

If these settling basins were the subject of Josephus's original description of the siting of the Roman rampart, then, in building "over against the middle" of them, the soldiers were erecting their embankment, very understandably, in the angle between the north wall of Antonia and the eastern side of the northwest tower.

Doubtless it was by making use of this canal connecting directly with the subterranean double cistern that John of Gischala, the Jewish rebel leader of whom we shall have much to say later, was able to undermine "the ground from Antonia right up to the earthworks, supporting the tunnel with props, and thus leaving the Roman works suspended" (JW V xi 4; §469). Unwittingly, the Romans had chosen a position for their rampart alongside an underground passage leading from the heart of the enemy's stronghold! Thus Josephus's studied reference to the "basin(s) of the Pool" was particularly relevant to the military situation. Later, the ground under the Roman engines attacking Antonia collapsed "at the point where John in his designs on the former earthworks had dug beneath it" (JW VI i 3; §28). That occurred on the twentieth of July, A.D. 70, and a few days later, Antonia taken, the Romans were able to penetrate into the Temple itself "through the mine excavated by John to reach their earthworks" (JW VI i 7; §71). This presumably means that the soldiers entered the double cistern from the aqueduct and carried on through a conduit dug in the southern wall toward the Temple area. In fact they could not have penetrated the whole way in this fashion, for, as modern exploration has shown, that passage was already blocked by the north wall of Herod's Temple platform.

CHAPTER TEN

The name by which Josephus speaks of the valley running through the center of the city area has always been a problem. He calls it the "Valley of the Cheesemakers" (*tōn turopoiōn*), whence it has been usually referred to (somewhat ungrammatically) as the Tyropoeon Valley (Figure 8). But the name is strange, if only that one would hardly expect such a pastoral occupation to have given its name to the center of a city. Again, until the opening of the copper scroll, we had never seen the Hebrew name for this valley. It was apparently entirely lacking from the Old Testament, which is very surprising when one considers what an important part this central depression played in the development and fortification of the city. Thanks to our scroll we now not only know the name but can recognize its existence in a somewhat corrupted form in the Bible. Item 35 reads:

In the Outer Valley, in the middle of the circle (?) upon (or, by) the Stone, buried at seventeen cubits under it: 17 talents of silver and gold.

Although no valley of this name is otherwise attested for Jerusalem, Isaiah speaks of a certain "valley of vision" (Isa. 22:1, 5), which can now be traced to a corruption of our word "outer." Furthermore, commentators have long sought to identify Isaiah's valley with this central depression, since a number of his topographical references point in that direction. Thus, "the waters of the lower pool" and the "reservoir between the two walls for the water of the old pool" (Isa. 22:9, 10) have been shown to suit the water system whose traces can still be recognized at the southern end of the Tyropoeon Valley (Figure 10).

Again Josephus's redactors have been at fault and have confused two different Semitic roots. That lying behind our "outer" is exactly similar to another meaning "congeal," and is used in Aramaic for the curdling of milk, or cheesemaking.

If "Outer Valley" seems a strange designation for a valley which cuts through the center of the city, it should be remembered that in ancient times only the southeastern knoll was inhabited, its northern part being known in the Old Testament as Ophel. This was the Jebusite city captured by David and refortified, and the "Outer Valley" would have played a very important part in the defense of its western flank.

The "circle upon the Stone" of our text is very unclear respecting the first word, but if true has a quaint Arthurian touch about it. Indeed, the legend to which it may relate is strongly reminiscent of the Round Table. Once upon a time, so we are told in Jewish folklore, there lived a very pious man called Onias the Circle-maker. His speciality was rain making, and his fame spread far and wide. Once, when Jerusalem was in the throes of a terrible drought, Onias was called in to hasten the longed-for rains. Willingly he came and, having drawn the circle which was apparently a necessary part of his ritual, commenced to pray hard for rain. At once large drops began to fall, to the delight of the populace. This continued for some time, the rain becoming heavier and heavier until the citizens began to worry about the danger of flooding and, taking refuge on the Temple mount, implored Onias to temper his enthusiasm with moderation. Before transmitting this plea to Heaven, however, Onias told the people to "go and see if the Stone of the Strayers has disappeared." Whatever this stone was, it could apparently act as a floodwater mark, which indicates that it must have stood in the middle of a wadi bed. If, as tradition has it, its name derived from its standing within the city as a place to which lost property might be brought for reclaiming, there was only one watercourse suitable for its location, the so-called Tyropoeon, or Outer Valley. Since the people were on the Temple mount at the time of Onias' request, the stone will have stood somewhere beneath its western wall, and the most suitable and central position could well have been under one of the bridges which connected the Temple mount to the southwestern hill.

It is not difficult to imagine such a legend as this growing up around a particularly conspicuous piece of rock in the valley bed, marked at the top by an incised circle and perhaps pierced through the center. It is not at all improbable, either, that it had to do with some primitive rain-making ceremony, such as that possibly underlying the Feast of the Tabernacles. The depth of burial noted in our scroll, some twenty-five and a half feet, indicates a hewn shaft or tunnel, perhaps communicating with such a drainage system as has in fact been found beneath an ancient pavement skirting the Sanctuary's west wall (Figure 17).

Item 29 of the scroll can be located in about the same area:

In the dam (?) which is in the Bridge of the High Priest [. . .] nine [cubits (?)]: [. . .] talents.

Josephus speaks of a bridge across the Tyropoeon Valley connecting one of the western gates of the Temple mount, probably the Qiphonos Gate of Jewish tradition, with the king's palace (JA XV xi 5; §410; Figure 10). The "king's palace" is usually understood to mean that of the Maccabean princes which stood on the promontory of the southwest hill. Elsewhere Josephus groups the palaces of Agrippa II and Bernice with the house of Ananias the High Priest (JW II xvii 6; §427), so one presumes that this bridge across the valley led also to the high priest's residence and could thus be aptly called, with our scroll, "the Bridge of the High Priest."

It served also to connect the Temple with the Xystus, an arena whose name derived from its "polished" (*xustos*) flagstones. This public forum lay either in the valley bottom or on the lower slopes of the southwest hill, directly under the royal palace (JW II xvi 3; §344; Figure 10). At one stage in the Jewish Revolt, the two rival rebel leaders, John of Gischala and Simon bar Giora, erected themselves a tower on each end of the bridge, John "over the gates leading out above the Xystus" (JW VI iii 2; §191), and Simon on the Xystus side. Later on, when force of circumstances united the rivals against the common foe, they both stood with their supporters at the western end of the bridge, while the Roman general Titus harangued them from the other.

One of the greatest fruits of the heroic Survey by Captain Wilson and his associates was the discovery of the beginning of this bridge, now called Wilson's Arch (Figure 11 *a*, *b*). Its forty-two feet once spanned the deepest part of the Outer Valley, and Wilson suggested that the bed was originally dammed at this point. When the city expanded northward, the dam would have been pierced to allow passage between the newly created suburb in the north and the other parts of the city. Perhaps the gap was then bridged by a wooden structure which was later replaced by a stone bridge, part of the remains of which were still visible in the mid-nineteenth century and are presumably there to be seen today by anyone able to gain access through surface building levels and underlying debris to Wilson's Arch.

Below the arch, almost on a level with its springing, Wilson found a floor of hard concrete, the bed of a disused reservoir (Figure 11 b). Later exploration by Captain Warren, who sank a shaft through to the valley bottom, showed that this floor stood some seventy feet above the rock. However, at a depth of only twenty-four feet he came upon a level of broken masonry and other remains of a fallen arch and wall. This would appear to have been the point from which an earlier arch was rebuilt, but it was not possible to explore the full extent of this level. There is little doubt that, were a modern excavation possible, the remains would tell a more complete story and give a more accurate dating than was possible a century ago.

To the west of Wilson's Arch stretched a most complicated series of underground vaults, consisting of two parallel but unequal rows of vaulted chambers and, at a lower level, another series of rooms, one of which Warren thought of equal age to the walls of the Herodian Sanctuary. From the chambers of the northern viaduct access was obtained to a "secret passage" leading westward directly underneath the present roadway to the Chain Gate of the Haram (Figure 11 a). This passage was about twelve feet wide with a semicircular vault. Its crown stood about nine feet

93

below the level of the roadway. Warren was able to explore it continuously to a point about 220 feet from the Haram wall, but a further portion discovered later, in use as a water tank, suggested that it continued much farther, probably reaching the Citadel on the western side of the city. There is actually a record from a fifteenth-century witness of just such a secret passageway from the Sanctuary to the Citadel. Although attributed by that writer to King David, in actual fact it seems probable that the passage is later than the Herodian era. Its importance lies in the access that it gives now, and could give even more were it completely cleared, to much lower strata of subterranean Jerusalem than are at present accessible from the built-up areas of the surface city. Certainly more could be excavated at the western end: Warren records that about thirteen feet below the passage his party managed to squeeze into a vaulted chamber, the crown of the roof of which was more than forty feet below street level. They battered their way through its eastern wall to find themselves in another vaulted chamber which again gave access to a narrow passage, only two feet, six inches wide, along which Warren crawled for ten feet before finding his way blocked by fallen masonry. He feared to push his way any farther lest he bring down the buildings perched above this heap of rubble, but he concluded that these vaults may once have been the vestibule to a postern leading from the Upper City on the southwest hill into the Tyropoeon Valley.

This indefatigable officer, on learning that there were similar vaults lying to the north of the causeway and leading up to the Jaffa Gate, tried to explore them, "but the filth was too great to allow of one getting up into them, as they were used for the refuse and sewage of the houses round about."[1]

A further hazard to be faced by any would-be explorers of subterranean Jerusalem is illustrated by another passage from the same fascinating book:

Having traced the (secret) passage to a distance of 220 feet from the Sanctuary wall, we found a thin wall blocking up the passage; we broke through it, and dropped down about 6 feet into a continuation of it stopped up by a wall to west, but opening with a door to south; through this we crept and then saw light, and getting through into another chamber to south, we found ourselves in a donkey stable, the owner of which happened to be there, and he, on seeing us grimed with dirt, rushed out swearing he was followed by the Gins.[2]

To reach Wilson's Arch, the visitor must first find a way under the present Muslim Hall of Justice. Interestingly enough, this comparatively modern building cannot be far from the site of the ancient Jewish Council Chamber, associated by Josephus with the Xystus, or forum (JW V iv 2; §144; Figure 10) and with the bridge across the Tyropoeon, or Outer Valley. It may have been here that Jesus was condemned by the Sanhedrin (Luke 22:66), although Christian tradition never seems to have concerned itself with the place, probably because the variant accounts of the Gospels associated the event with the house of the high priest, Caiaphas.

Actually the site of the Council Chamber at the time of the Crucifixion is not clear, for Jewish tradition offers a number of different locations for it prior to this time, including one of the buildings bordering

[1] Charles Warren and Charles Wilson, *The Recovery of Jerusalem*, London: Richard Bentley & Son, 1871, p. 94.
[2] *Ibid.*, p. 90.

the southern boundary of the Temple's Inner Court. Around A.D. 30, however, it was moved into the city itself, presumably to the site by the bridge where Josephus locates it. Here, anyway, Peter, Stephen, and Paul were judged (Acts 4:5 f., 6:12, 22:30).

It seems to me that our scroll throws light on another of the problems concerning this Council Chamber, known in Jewish sources as "the Chamber of Hewn Stone" (*lishkath hag-gāzīth*). Other translations have been offered for this last phrase, but it is at least as possible philologically to read it as an alternative form of the Hebrew given by our scroll for "bridge" (*mᵉgīzah*). "Chamber of the Bridge" would have been very suitable for the Council's quarters in the Outer Valley, although, of course, quite anachronistic when referred to the chamber in the Inner Court of the Temple.

CHAPTER ELEVEN

The west and south of the city of Jerusalem is bordered by a valley called, in the Bible, "the Valley of Hinnom" or "the Valley of the Son(s) of Hinnom" (Figure 10). It always seems to have had particularly gruesome associations. Part of it, called Topheth or "hearth," was the place where the wicked kings Ahaz and Manasseh placated the god Molech by burning little children (II Kings 23:10; cf. Isa. 30:33). It was to be known as the Valley of Slaughter according to Jeremiah (Jer. 7:32, 19:6, 11), and in Jewish apocalyptic literature it became the place of punishment or hell for all apostates from Jewry, and so came into the New Testament as the place of eternal punishment, Graecized to *Gehenna* (Matt. 5:22, etc.).

The eastern end of the valley, on the south side, was localized as the traditional "Potter's Field," later called Hakeldama, or the Field of Blood. This was the ground said to have been purchased by Judas Iscariot with his thirty pieces of silver, and where he perished (Acts 1:18 f.), but which, according to Matthew, the chief priests bought with the returned money "to bury strangers in." An early Christian writer speaks of it as still having the smell of decay, so much so that the passer-by was obliged to hold his nose, and in the fourth century it was still used as a burial place for strangers.

Two items of the scroll refer to the Shaveh, which must also be sought to the south of the city:

37. In the stubble field of the Shaveh, facing southwest, in an underground passage looking north, buried at twenty-four cubits: 67 talents.

38. In the irrigation channel (?) of the Shaveh, in the constricted part (?) that is in it, buried at eleven cubits: 70 talents of silver.

It must be said at once that it is by no means certain whether the scribe here intends Shaveh to be read as a proper name or to mean simply "plain." Possibly because either is possible he is here willing to risk the proper name. It is certainly as a proper name that Shaveh occurs in Genesis 14:17 as the name of the valley or plain (*'ēmeq;* see above, p. 64) where the victorious Abram was met by the King of Sodom and was blessed by Melchizedek, "king of Salem." A later commentator has added the gloss that the Vale of Shaveh was the "King's Vale," which is reminiscent of the "King's Garden" through which Zedekiah escaped during a siege of Jerusalem by the Chaldeans (II Kings 25:4; cf. Jer. 39:4, 52:7). This garden lay at the south end of the southeastern hill, in the vicinity of the Pool of Siloam, so we should probably seek the biblical Shaveh at the southern end of the Tyropoeon, or Outer, Valley where it joins with the Hinnom and broadens out into a plain, or *'ēmeq.* Interestingly enough, this finds some confirmation in an old Aramaic version of Genesis which explains the Shaveh as the "Plain of Vision," thinking no doubt of Isaiah's "Valley of Vision" which, as we have seen (p. 89), really indicated our Outer, or Tyropoeon Valley.

The particular region referred to by our scroll apparently faced southwest, which must mean that the name Shaveh could be applied to the whole southern stretch of the Hinnom Valley, as far as the cistern called the Sultan's Pool (*birket es-sultān*). The field concerned will have been near the site of this reservoir, on the eastern bank of the valley, and thus "facing southwest." Precisely under this stretch of ground lie parts of the aqueduct which once brought water from Solomon's Pools at Etan (Figure 2) to the Temple area (JA XVIII iii 2; §60; JW II ix 4; §175). The aqueduct's course runs up by the western side of the Sultan's Pool, around its northern end, and then down this eastern stretch before curving round the southwestern corner of the city and across the Outer Valley to the Haram. Here is how Warren describes a stretch of this conduit shortly after it leaves our location:

On the open ground on the western hill which lies south of the city wall, we made an important discovery, viz., an ancient aqueduct, at the south-east corner of the Coenaculum, and about 50 feet north of the present aqueduct—I have no doubt that it must be the original aqueduct from Solomon's Pools to the Sanctuary. We dug out the earth from a stone shaft 2 feet square, and at a depth of 16 feet was a channel running from the west to the north-east, precisely similar in construction to the passages under the Triple Gate. It varies very much in size; sometimes we could crawl on hands and knees, then we have to creep sideways, again we lay on our backs and wriggled along, but still it was always large enough for a man of ordinary dimensions. In parts built of masonry, in parts cut out of solid rock, it is generally of a semi-cylindrical shape; but in many parts it has the peculiar shoulders which I have seen only under the Triple Gateway, but which has been noticed by Mr. Eaten, in the channel leading towards Tekoa. To the north-east we traced the channel for 250 feet, until we were stopped by a shaft which was filled with earth; to the west we traced it for 200 feet, till it was stopped in the same manner. In part of this passage we could stand upright, it being 10 or 12 feet high, with the remains of two sets of stones for covering, as shown in M. Piazzi Smyth's work on the Great Pyramid; the stones at the sides being of great size—12 feet by 6. This channel is evidently of ancient construction. It is built in lengths as though the work had been commenced at several points, and had not been directed correctly. The plaster is in good preservation.

The aqueduct was traced for 700 feet, and at either end it was found to be crossed and used by the present low level aqueduct, it being at the same level, but the entrances are much farther up the hill on account of the cutting being so deep, in one place 29 feet below the present surface.

It is apparent that the builder of the present low level aqueduct made use of the original one wherever it was convenient.[1]

Presumably we should look for a shaft coming to the surface at the south end of the north-south stretch, similar to the one Warren describes hewn out of the rock to a depth of sixteen feet. It is from this point, probably, that the scroll's "twenty-four cubits," about thirty-six feet, should be measured toward the north. As elsewhere in the scroll, where the scribe is locating treasure buried in an underground passage of some kind, the distance at which it was concealed has to be measured *along* the passage, not buried at that depth under solid rock or earth.

Unfortunately, the following item, 38, is far from clear, mainly because the technical items allow a number of different interpretations. It seems probable, however, that the deposit was made in or about the valley's irrigation system and has possibly to do with

[1] Warren and Wilson, *The Recovery of Jerusalem*, pp. 233 ff.

the pool or dam which once lay on the site of the medieval cistern, now known as the Sultan's Pool. Almost certainly this neck of the valley would have been utilized in some such way for irrigation and water conservation in the first century, and the present cistern's predecessor may well have been the so-called Serpents' Pool located about here by Josephus (JW V iii 2; §108). The place called *Bethso* by the historian (JW V iv 2; §145), hitherto unidentified but clearly lying in this area, perhaps preserves the "Shaveh" of our scroll (i.e., Beth ["House, Place of"] Shaveh).

CHAPTER TWELVE

Of all the valleys that run through and around Jerusalem, it is the Kidron that is richest in religious and historical associations (Figure 12). It separates the Temple mount from Olivet and was once very much deeper than it is today. For centuries it has been the city's rubbish dump and even now serves as a sewer. The resultant accumulation of rubble has disguised the considerable gulf that once defended the city's eastern wall which goes down probably another eighty feet below the present surface (Figure 13).

King David had to cross this ravine when he fled from the city toward the wilderness (II Sam. 15:23). Jesus crossed it in the same direction, going to the Mount of Olives and "a garden" of which we shall have to speak later.

The eastern bank of the Kidron was used as a necropolis for the city from the earliest times, and until very recently, pious Jews the world over arranged for their mortal remains to be buried here to await their resurrection within sight of the walls of the Holy City. It was here that the common graves were situated in biblical times (II Kings 23:6; cf. Jer. 26:23), and probably where we should see another common grave:

55. In the grave of the common people of pure life (?) there are vessels for tithe or tithe of [. . .], arranged side by side (?).

Unfortunately, where exactly along the valley such common graves were situated we have at present no means of knowing. More precise are the directions given in our scroll for finding another tomb:

52. Below the Portico's southern corner, in the Tomb of Zadok, under the pillar of the exedra: vessels of tithe of [. . .] and tithe of [. . .], arranged side by side (?).

The Portico, needing apparently no further definition, can hardly be other than the double-columned arcade running along the eastern side of the Temple area, just above the eastern city wall (Figure 14). It seems to have been a favorite meeting place, its roof nearly forty feet high, paneled inside with cedar, affording shelter in the wintry weather. It was here that Jesus taught during the Feast of Dedication and where His compatriots sought to stone Him because He would not lead them into bloody revolution (John 10:23 f.). It was here, too, that the disciples gathered after His death, preaching and performing signs and miracles (Acts 3:11, 5:12).

The popular ascription of this magnificent construction to Solomon, shared even by Josephus (JA XX ix 7; §221; cf. VIII iii 9; §98; XV xi 3; §398 f.; JW V v 1; §185), is certainly wrong, although King Herod's architects may well have utilized parts of earlier building in their grand design.

Porticoes ran also round the other sides of the Temple court, but our reference to a tomb beneath "the Portico's southern corner" can only mean on the eastern side since a tomb within the city walls would not have been permitted.

At the southern end of this arcade there reared up the Pinnacle of the Temple, some three hundred feet or more from the bedrock of the ravine (Plate 30).

Thus Josephus describes its terrifying effect on anyone looking down from its summit:

For while the depth of the ravine was great, and no one who bent over to look into it from above could bear to look down to the bottom, the height of the Portico standing over it was so very great that if anyone looked down from its rooftop, combining the two elevations, he would become dizzy and his vision would be unable to reach the end of so measureless a depth (JA XV xi 5; §412).

It was from here that Jesus was tempted to throw Himself down, confident that God would protect Him from harm (Matt. 4:5; Luke 4:9).

As recent excavations have confirmed, the southeast corner of the Muslim Sanctuary, or Haram, rests on the lower courses of the Herodian walls, so we can accurately locate the position of the tomb referred to by our scroll. The text's "below" is actually a compound preposition in Hebrew, literally "from below," indicating a position not directly beneath the corner but some way removed from it.

Sure enough, on a line with the southeastern corner and extending some way to the north are a series of tombs. They date between the second century B.C. and the first century A.D. and are popularly attributed to Jehoshaphat, Absalom, St. James, and Zechariah (Plate 31; Figures 12, 15). There is also an unfinished sepulcher to the south of Zechariah which is almost on a direct line with a prolongation of the south wall of the Haram eastward, and this fits better than the others the position indicated by the scroll for "the tomb of Zadok."

On our expedition we made an excavation here and around the base of the Zechariah monument to find out just how well these features fitted the topography of the copper scroll. It was soon apparent that the small unnamed tomb was intended to be a replica of the St. James sepulcher a little to the north. This is, in fact, a complex of tombs cut back into the hillside of the Mount of Olives, having a two-pillared façade before a covered porch, or exedra, of pure Doric form. On the architrave of the porch is carved an inscription in Hebrew giving the names of those buried within, priests of the family of Hezir. This epitaph was written about two generations after the first burial and can be dated paleographically to the end of the pre-Christian era.

The origin of the popular ascription of the tomb to St. James is obscure. But interestingly enough, at least one James, "the brother of the Lord," is connected with this area in legend. He was said to have been thrown down from the Pinnacle by his Jewish enemies and stoned. This is the story as recounted by Eusebius, quoting the second-century Christian authority Hegesippus:

They came, therefore, and set James on the Pinnacle of the Temple and cried to him, "O thou Just One, to whom we are all bound to listen, tell us what is the Door of Jesus." And he answered with a loud voice, "Why do ye ask me concerning Jesus the Son of Man? He is both seated in heaven on the right hand of power and he will come again on the clouds of heaven." And when many were convinced and gave glory at the witness of James, the same scribes and Pharisees said to each other, "We have done ill in bringing forward such a testimony to Jesus; let us go up and cast him down, that they may fear to believe him." And they cried out saying, "Alas! even the Just has gone astray." And they fulfilled that which is written in Isaiah, "Let us take away the Just, for he is not for our purpose." So they cast down James the Just, and

PLATE 18. Examining the earthquake rift in the cistern of Khirbet Qumran.

PLATE 19. Part of the silver treasure hoard discovered at Khirbet Qumran.

PLATE 20. Making a sounding at the western end of the Hall of Congregation, Qumran.

PLATE 21. Across the Wadi Kelt toward Taurus, seen from Cypros ("Mount Gerizim").

PLATE 22. Looking from the Wadi Kelt northward toward the site of Alexandreion.

PLATE 23. The outline of the Herodian fortress of Cypros from the slope of the hill.

PLATE 24. Searching the cistern in Cypros.

PLATE 25. The Mount of Temptation *(Docus)*, looking over the tell of ancient Jericho.

PLATE 26. Part of the excavations of Bethesda in the grounds of St. Anne's.

PLATE 27. One of the Antonia cisterns under the Sisters of Zion Convent.

PLATE 28. The chamber at the north end of the Antonia double cistern.

PLATE 29. The upper Kidron Valley as it leaves Jerusalem.

PLATE 30. The southeastern corner of the Haram, site of the Pinnacle of the Temple, seen from the porch of St. James's tomb across the valley.

PLATE 31. The ancient Jewish tombs at the foot of the Mount of Olives: Absalom, St. James, Zechariah, and "Zadok"

PLATE 32. Excavating the "Zadok" tomb.

PLATE 33. Part of the lower Kidron ("Wadi of Fire") with the Mar Saba monastery.

PLATE 34. The Golden Gate, Jerusalem.

they began to stone him since he was not killed by the fall; but he kneeled down, saying, "O Lord God, my Father, I beseech thee forgive them, for they know not what they do." While they were thus stoning him, one of the priests of the sons of Rechab, of whom Jeremiah the prophet testifies, cried out, "Stop! What do ye? The Just is praying for you." But one of them, who was a fuller, smote the head of the Just One with his club. And so he bore his witness. And they buried him on the spot, and his monument still stands by the side of the Temple with the inscription, "He hath been a true witness both to Jews and Greeks that Jesus is the Christ."

Much of this story is probably quite fictitious, or at least a mixture of different traditions, and indeed this important pillar of the first Church is altogether a mysterious figure, not least in his relationship with Jesus and the disciples. What is interesting about the story from our point of view is that the place where he was reputed to have been stoned coincides with that given by our scroll for the "Tomb of Zadok," and furthermore, that he was surnamed The Just, which in Hebrew would be *Zaddik* or perhaps *Zadduk,* either of which could correspond with the name I have conventionally rendered as Zadok. Josephus has a more sober and probably truer account of James's death: that he and some others were tried before the Sanhedrin, charged with breaking the laws, and (illegally) executed by stoning (JA XX ix 1; §200). Could it be that the Hegesippus account arose through the association of the well-known Temptation story and the presence of a tomb below the Pinnacle, already popularly ascribed to one surnamed The Just, or Zadok?

Our scroll tells us a little more about this Tomb of Zadok and the cliff out of which it was hewn:

53. In the treading place (?) at the top of the cliff facing west, in front of the Garden of Zadok, under the great sealing stone that is in its outlet: consecrated offerings (*hērem*).

The westward-facing cliff suits our Hellenistic tombs well, and it now seems that this particular tomb was furnished with a courtyard or "garden" in front of it. A road runs directly under the cliff in which the St. James tomb is situated, but the Zechariah monument stands back somewhat and during our excavations we were able to clear the ground in front of the huge monolith. There we did, in fact, discover a courtyard and to our surprise found that there had been a chamber at some time dug into the pedestal of the monument (Figure 15). From the back of the little chamber a crack in the rock exuded a trickle of water. Doubtless before the construction of the modern tarmac road farther up the side of Olivet drained the rainwater off to the north, much more seeped into the hillside and found its way out through crevices in the rock at the foot of the mount. This seems to be confirmed by our discovery of a roughly hewn conduit from the sill of the little chamber out through the courtyard to the edge of the platform. It was perhaps meant to lead water into a cistern below, still buried beneath many feet of debris.

This scroll reference and our archaeological findings are the first indication that these ancient sepulchers had "gardens" or "courtyards" in front of them, and raises some very interesting questions about the true whereabouts of the Garden of the Agony, or Gethsemane.

Tradition since the fourth century has placed the Garden higher up the Mount of Olives to the north of the scroll treasure cache, and today the visitor has no less than three highly revered Gethsemanes to choose from. But these sitings depend on the mistaken assumption that Jesus would have left the city by the eastern gate of the Sanctuary, which lay near the position of the present Golden Gate (see below, p. 119). In fact, as Jewish tradition makes clear, that exit would certainly not have been used as a public thoroughfare. If the events of the day before the Crucifixion took place in the lower city, as seems most probable, a southerly gate would have been more convenient for an approach to the Mount of Olives. Whether Jesus used a gate in the eastern wall or walked round from one of the gates in the south of the city, His direct path when "He went forth with His disciples across the Kidron Valley, where there was a garden" (John 18:1) would have led Him by the Garden of Zadok.

Dare we identify the copper scroll's Garden of Zadok, or the Just One, with the Garden of the Agony? All one can say for certain is that Christian tradition seems to have found this area beneath the Pinnacle, scene of the Temptation and of the death of the Lord's brother, of particular interest. Again, if the Garden were connected with a tomb, it does at least give a reason for there being a garden on the Mount of Olives at all, a feature of the Gospel narrative which has always caused commentators some difficulty, and led to forced speculations on the ownership and function of a garden in the middle of olive orchards.

We have another reference in the New Testament to a "garden tomb," that of Joseph of Arimathea, the rich disciple of Jesus (John 19:41, etc.). It was there that Jesus was laid after the Crucifixion, and it is described as "a new tomb where no one had ever been laid," close by the place of Crucifixion. Its location depends, therefore, on the true site of Golgotha, a question that has perhaps raised more storms of emotion and personal bitterness among scholars than any other aspect of New Testament topography. The cold facts are that despite all the wishful thinking of the protagonists, we just do not know where this place of execution was except that it lay outside the city, near a cemetery, and by a thoroughfare leading from the country (Matt. 27:32 ff., etc.). The site marked by the decrepit Church of the Holy Sepulcher goes back certainly to the fourth century but has no more real claim to authenticity than any of the many other locations marked out for Golgotha. It suffers, furthermore, from very real doubts about the course of the old "second wall" of the Roman city and the possibility that it did not exclude this site, in which case, of course, it could not possibly have been a place of execution.

One can only say that if Joseph were rich enough, the place he would have chosen above all for his family sepulcher would have been in the vicinity of the scroll's Tomb of Zadok, on the west-facing lower slopes of the Mount of Olives. If it was in the funerary garden of his rich disciple that Jesus went on the night of His betrayal it would account for His being able to make free use of such a private enclosure near a public thoroughfare.

Whether, in the first century, there was some feature about our "cliff facing west" that made it look like a skull (if this is what earned for it the name Golgotha), we cannot know, but certainly as far as being a place of execution, James was believed to have been killed there, and the Kidron Valley has always had the sinister reputation of a place of judgment. It was, furthermore, outside the city wall and near a track along the Kidron leading to "the country."

Is it even possible that our "Tomb of Zadok" was Joseph's garden sepulcher? Our excavations showed that the construction of the small unnamed tomb just to the south of the Zechariah monument had proceeded no further than a rough hewing out of the pillars supporting the roof of the porch (Plate 32). Sufficient rock had been cut away behind to allow a body to be laid in the entrance (a skeleton was, in fact, found lying there, feet to the sill) but work had ceased abruptly. We could see where the mason's chisel had dug round a slab of rock preparatory to breaking it off, but his hand had been stayed by some dramatic event at which we can now only guess. It may have been an earthquake, for the pillars are cracked through and the roof of the little porch had collapsed. The crack can be seen running right across the Zechariah monolith, and, as we discovered, this too had been left unfinished.

It was long ago suggested that the description of Joseph's tomb as "new" might have meant "unfinished," but it would be difficult to fit other details of the Passion story into the kind of tomb we excavated. The open porch of the "Zadok tomb" hardly allows of sealing by a rolling stone, for instance. Nevertheless, it was interesting to note that next door to the unfinished portico was a single burial chamber hewn back into the rock with an entrance only some two feet square.

Incidentally, from the point of view of the treasure deposit, although the cliff below the unfinished tomb "exedra" had been extensively cut about in later times, it was just possible to recognize the inner end of another of these small tomb niches that had run back into the rock face and ended up at a point very nearly "under the pillar."

In proposing these possibilities of identification of the scroll's treasure caches with the most important features of New Testament sacred topography, we have, of course, strayed well into the field of conjecture in matters that do not allow of any degree of certainty. The contemporary witness of the copper scroll undoubtedly offers more authentic details about the funerary installations of this important area than anything we have had hitherto, but the information given us by the Gospels is so sparse there is really very little chance of our ever discovering for certain the exact location of the Garden of the Agony or of Joseph's tomb and Golgotha.

Nevertheless, if it were true that our "Tomb of Zadok" had been thirty years previously the temporary resting place of the Christian Messiah, the continued ascription to it of the name or title *Zadduk* is in keeping with the New Testament record of Jesus' title among the Apostles, "The Just" or "Righteous One" (Acts 3:14, 7:52, 22:14). It would also imply that this title and identification was more widespread among the populace than hitherto believed likely, to the extent that a generation after Jesus's death one particular spot was still locally recognized as being associated with the Nazarene Master.

CHAPTER THIRTEEN

After leaving the city of Jerusalem, the Kidron Valley winds its way for some twenty miles toward the Dead Sea. It runs first in a southeasterly direction and then turns eastward, carving deep gorges through the folds of the Judaean hills. In its lower reaches it is called locally the *Wadi en-Nār*, the Wadi of Fire, recalling perhaps the associations with eternal judgment of its upper course, but in any case graphically describing its sun-scorched bed during the summer months. For most of the year it is quite dry, and the sun beats relentlessly into the gorges, bleaching the rocks into a dazzling whiteness and driving life into the shelter of the thousands of caves that pit the cliffs on either side (Plate 33).

It was along this route that, each Day of Atonement, the Jews used to drive the scapegoat laden with the sins of the people (Lev. 16). The desert was reckoned to begin some three miles from the city, and the gorge into which the wretched animal was cast, to be broken in pieces before it reached the bottom, was called a *tsōq*, and lay about twelve miles from Jerusalem. Interestingly enough the one mention we have by name of the Kidron in our scroll also refers to a gorge or precipice, using the same Hebrew word:

36. In the dam (?) at the mouth of the Kidron gorge (*tsōq*), buried at three cubits: 7 talents.

113

Just where the scapegoat was ritually slaughtered in this fashion we do not know but must presume it was some well-defined constriction in the Kidron Valley as must have been our treasure cache. Today the most striking of the gorges of the Wadi of Fire is that sheltering the ancient monastery of Mar Saba (see above, pp. 54 ff.; Figure 4). This lies only about nine or ten miles from the city, however, measured along the valley. A reckoning of twelve miles made as the crow flies brings us very near to the Dead Sea, to the final gorges before the valley breaks through onto the coastal plain, with a last terrifying drop of some hundreds of feet. A few miles short of this, not long after the wadi begins its final twisting course through high-walled cliffs, is the site of Christmas Cave where a small scrolls expedition led by myself in recent years sought and found evidence of habitation in the early centuries of our era (see *Search in the Desert*).

This is certainly one of the most exciting and promising archaeological hunting grounds of all Palestine. The Kidron Valley must have been an important escape route from Jerusalem from the earliest times. In three miles anybody seeking the anonymity of the wilderness would be safe. Throughout its length, caves offered the refugee shelter and hiding, as we found strikingly illustrated in our Christmas Cave, where Jewish warriors and their families must have taken refuge during the years of the second Jewish Revolt of the second century of our era.

Most tempting of all the possibilities offered by this area is perhaps the discovery of relics of the first Christian community who fled from the city in about A.D. 68. Then the Jewish followers of Jesus who formed the Mother Church disappeared from Jerusalem and virtually from history, taking their priceless records with them. Thereafter the central control of the Church swung outside Palestine and Gentile Christianity was given fresh and decisive impetus. The more restrictive religion of the Jewish Church perished with it and the saving faith of Paul and his friends allowed to flourish outside the realms of Judaism. But with the Mother Church went its written records, collections of proof texts, the sayings of Jesus and the like; documents which, were they ever to be found, would bring a new and perhaps revolutionary outlook on Christian beginnings.

It seems not improbable that these Jewish-Christians fled by way of the Kidron and then crossed over into the country of the ancient Moabites, or found their way south to the Red Sea and thus to Egypt. But if they came this way they would certainly have found refuge in caves in the Kidron gorges, and some may have decided to stay and await the end of the world and the Second Coming which the terrible war with the Romans must surely presage.

The presence of the Mar Saba monastery and other similar Christian settlements in the vicinity four centuries later may possibly point to a tradition lingering around the Kidron that the ground had already been hallowed by early followers of the Galilean Teacher.

CHAPTER FOURTEEN

One of the few undisputed features of the topography of first-century Jerusalem is the situation of the Temple area. It lay on the upper part of the southeastern hill and covered most of the present-day Muslim sacred area, or Haram (Figure 8). The actual rock formation below the present platform is still incompletely known, for the only place where bedrock is visible is in the center of the great octagonal building which commands the whole Sanctuary, the Dome of the Rock (*PDSS* Plate 88). Scholars usually identify this Rock (*es-Sakhra*) with the site of the Altar of King Solomon's Temple, which was followed after the Jewish Exile by the temples of Zerubbabel and lastly Herod the Great. The last was but an embellishment of the second, so that the edifice standing in Jesus' time is usually referred to as the Second Temple (Figures 14, 16).

In all, I think some two dozen of the scroll's locations are situated within the Temple area, but these have been carefully distributed among other locations, doubtless for purposes of secrecy. Only persons having an intimate knowledge of the Temple courts and their chambers, their private names and functions, would be able to recognize them and rob them of their sacred treasure. It can be imagined, therefore, that our task, twenty centuries after their destruction, is not an easy one. The calamity of A.D. 70 when the Romans razed the Temple area, followed after centuries of neglect by its reoccupation as a Muslim sanctuary, has destroyed many of its most conspicuous landmarks. Nevertheless, thanks largely to Josephus and rabbinic tradition, the case is by no means hopeless. Surprisingly many of the most intimate details of the Herodian Temple and its chambers have been preserved; indeed, it is often the case that the functions and inner detail of the various ancillary buildings have been remembered while their general layout still presents intractable problems. These are partly the result of inconsistency between Josephus and the rabbis, and there is a suspicion that the latter depend rather more on the picture of the ideal Temple as portrayed by Ezekiel than on historical fact. These inconsistencies are not, however, of urgent moment for our researches into the copper scroll: we are more concerned with the inner details of the rooms and their subterranean passageways than their relative topography, and it is here that our Jewish sources are of the greatest assistance. Foremost among these is the collection of traditions known as the Mishnah, dating in its edited form from the middle of the second century A.D., but containing customs and laws going back at least four centuries. This work is written in a Hebrew dialect closely related to that of our scroll and contains a wealth of technical terms which are particularly valuable (see Chapter Two). Furthermore, Temple chambers and water installations are mentioned there by names which must have been common knowledge to those working within the Temple service but practically unknown to an outsider, just as members of a college or cathedral close will have their own private names for its gates, stairways, passages, and so on, which would never appear in standard works of reference. With our scroll before us, we have then to try and reconstruct from such names the functions of the various installations, where these are not made explicit, and to seek the original names which underlie our scribe's pseudonyms.

Entrance into the Sanctuary on the eastern side was made through one special gate used by all the great religious processionals between the Temple and the Mount of Olives. Particular sanctity attached to this entrance so that it was only natural, if probably quite unhistoric, that Christian tradition should fasten on it as the point of Jesus' triumphal entry on Palm Sunday. Today the bricked-up Golden Gate stands in about the same position (Figures 13, 14; Plate 34), and gains its name from an old misunderstanding of the Greek *horaia,* "beautiful," of Acts 3:2 (= *aurea,* "golden"!) which was applied to another gate entirely, inside the Temple mount. The Golden Gate in its present form goes back no further than the sixth century A.D. but it may reutilize elements from the older entrance, which was probably a double gate of much the same construction. What the original looked like can be seen in its contemporary built into the southern wall of the Haram (Figure 13). Its sill will have stood at about the same height from the ground outside, and within there was a gatehouse with a ramp communicating with the higher level of the platform itself. In the case of the Golden Gate, the ground from the sill slopes up some twenty-three feet to the platform.

This gate and its chamber may be the reference of Item 26 of our scroll:

[In] the cavity of the pillar of the Double Gate, facing east, [in] the northern entrance, buried at three [cu]bits, (hidden) there is a pitcher; in it, one scroll, under it 42 talents.

It was through the eastern gate that the high priest and his party went forth to the Mount of Olives during the ceremony of burning the Red Heifer (Num. 19:2 f.). Interestingly enough, the word used by our scribe for "pitcher" coincides with that found in rabbinic tradition for the vessel containing the ashes of the sacrifice. Whether a cavity beneath the sill of the northern doorway of this very special Temple entrance was a recognized storage place for the sacred pitcher, we do not know, but it seems quite probable. In this case, the "scroll" hidden within it may have been a copy of the Law used during the ceremony. In the rabbinic tractate dealing with the regulations for the Red Heifer ceremony, there is a section concerned with the question of whether contact between a biblical scroll and the pitcher used for the sacrificial ashes affected the ritual cleanliness of the latter.

Captain Warren tried desperately hard to reach the Haram wall below the Golden Gate to confirm, among other things, the originality or otherwise of its position. The Muslim cemetery immediately in front of it prevented his sinking a shaft down the face of the wall, so that he was obliged to dig it some distance away and tunnel underground toward the Haram. The nearest acceptable place was found to be no less than 143 feet distant from the Gate (Figure 17). At that point the ground level was already over fifty-five feet below the sill, and he sank his shaft a further twenty-five feet before driving the tunnel horizontally inward. He had gone a little over ten feet when he struck the solid rock of the valley floor, and this the party followed as it rose toward the Haram, at an angle of one-in-four. They passed a rock-hewn tomb or cistern eight and a half feet farther on and climbed a rock scarp in which a ring had been cut for tethering animals. Rubble walls now confronted them, but they broke through without too much difficulty and were brought to a halt only by a massive masonry wall. After penetrating five feet through its stonework, they gave up and turned along its face southward, until loose debris threatened to engulf the party if they continued. Nothing daunted, they returned along their tunnel and tried again in a different direction to reach the Haram. Again the masonry wall confronted them, and this time they followed its face northward, only to run once more into the loose shingle. There was nothing left now but to give up the project entirely, so that to this day we cannot be sure of the original line of the Herodian Temple wall at this point or the original position of the Golden Gate. When Warren abandoned his attempts, his party, consisting mainly of native workmen using the most primitive tools, were still over fifty-five feet below ground and had tunneled altogether one hundred and eighty feet through the most treacherous soil. Here is how Warren describes the project:

It was disagreeable to have failed in reaching the Golden Gate, but to pierce through the debris of the nature encountered, some special machinery would have to be used; and it was dangerous to put anything but the simplest instruments into the hands of the fellahīn.

We also could not work more than a certain number of days at a time at a difficult place, as the constant danger caused the nerves to become unstrung after a time, and then a few days at safer work was required; only those who have experienced the peculiar effect of the rattling of debris upon the frames, with the prospect at any moment of the boards being crushed in by a large stone, can appreciate the deterring influence it had upon the workmen. The non-commissioned officers had to keep continually to the front, or the men would not venture up.

It appears probable that the massive wall met with may continue up to the surface, as immediately above it, in the road, are some large roughly-bevelled stones lying in the same line.[1]

Once inside the great double gate in the east wall, the procession would have entered the Outer Court, surrounded, as we have seen, by pillared arcades (see above, p. 104). In our scroll this is probably the reference of the "Court of the Peristyle" or "Colonnade" of Item 3:

In the Great Cistern which is in the Court of the Peristyle, in the spout in its floor, concealed in a hole in front of the upper opening: nine hundred talents.

The Mishnah actually speaks of one of the Temple cisterns as "the Great Cistern," and this term occurs again in a broken passage in Item 16 of the inventory:

In the Great Cistern which is in [. . .], in a pillar in its north: [. . .] talents.

The apocryphal book of Ecclesiasticus, or the Wisdom of Jesus, the Son of Sirach, mentions a particularly large reservoir that was built in the Temple area about 200 B.C. by the pious High Priest Simon, son of Onias, and which may be the same "Great Cistern": "In his days a water-reservoir was cut, a basin with a circumference like a sea" (50:3).

The Survey officers located and mapped those underground water installations of the Sanctuary that communicated with the surface (Figure 17), and if

[1] Warren and Wilson, *The Recovery of Jerusalem,* pp. 158 f.

the name "Great Cistern" meant the largest of all the reservoirs in the Temple area, we may perhaps identify it with Tank No. 8 of the Survey plans, described thus:

Usually known as the "Great Sea," (it) is called by the natives *Bir el-Aswad* or "Black Well." It is a fine cavern with rocky piers, reached from the south by a narrow staircase. It is 43 feet deep, being partly roofed in rock and partly with flat stones. It is the largest of all the Sanctuary tanks, and has numerous manholes from the surface, three of which are in use. The floor, where visible (when the water is low), consists of a sort of limestone shingle. The rock surface is at the level 2,411 or 5 feet beneath the present surface. A conduit enters this tank from the east. On the north-east there is a small circular chamber. The capacity of this tank is at least two million gallons.[2]

Perhaps one of the piers supporting the roof is the "pillar" referred to in Item 16, and the conduit from the east that is spoken of in Item 17:

In the water conduit which enters [. . .] as you go in four [. . .] cubits: 40 talents of silver [in] a chest (?).

[2] C. Warren and C. R. Conder, *The Survey of Western Palestine, Jerusalem,* London: Palestine Exploration Fund, 1884, pp. 219 f.

CHAPTER FIFTEEN

Within the Sanctuary area the ground was divided into a number of reservations (Figure 14). Non-Jews were allowed into the outermost of these courts but could not go nearer the central area than a low balustrade set with warning notices in Greek and Latin. Two of these have been found, and read:

Strangers are forbidden to pass the barrier and enter the precincts of the Sanctuary. Anyone found doing so will himself be responsible for the death penalty which will be inflicted on him.

This restrictive barrier and dire warning explains the scene recorded in the Book of Acts when Paul was accused of bringing foreigners into the Temple and thus defiling the holy place (21:28).

The space within this balustrade Josephus refers to as the "second enclosure," and here were the inner courts of the Temple itself. These were reserved for women, men, and priests in that ascending order of precedence. On the western side of the innermost court was the Temple itself and in front of its entrance, the great Altar.

The Women's Court was so called, not because it was exclusively reserved for women, but because they were not allowed to go beyond that point, probably for reasons of ritual purity, involving menstruation, childbirth and so on. According to the Mishnah, small unroofed enclosures had been made at each of its four corners and were used for various purposes. One was where the Nazarites cut off their hair and burned it under the pot in which the peace offering was cooking (Num. 6:17, 18). Another was called the Chamber of the Lepers, and another was used to store wine and oil. The fourth of these small chambers is of particular interest to us. It was situated in the northeast of the Court and was used to store wood. There priests who were ritually unfit to take part in the sacrificial worship of the Temple had the duty of examining the altar fuel for worms which would render it unfit to be burned in the sacrifice. Item 8 of our scroll says:

In the cistern that is within the underground passage which is in the Court of Wood Stores there are vessels and seventy talents of silver.

The eastern entrance into the set of inner courts was an impressive gateway made of Corinthian bronze, and is probably the one that the New Testament names "Beautiful," where the cripple sat begging alms "of those who entered the Temple" (Acts 3:2, 10). On the far side of the Women's Court where a semicircular staircase of fifteen steps led up into the Court of Israel was a "far larger" gate, called Nicanor, and overlaid with silver and gold (Figure 16; JW V v 3; §205). This was probably the site of the so-called Threshold of the Temple referred to in the Book of Ezekiel: ". . . and water was issuing from below the threshold of the temple toward the east" (Ezek. 47:1), and is the reference of Item 10 of our scroll:

In the cistern that is under the wall on the east, in a spur of rock: six pitchers of silver; its entrance is under the Great Threshold.

This same gateway is probably also the site of the entrance (*'ithōn*) to the Temple mentioned in Ezekiel's vision (40:15) and it is the same, rather special word, that our scribe uses to describe the site of the Treasury in Item 34:

[In the drain]pipe which is in the eastern path to the Treasury, which is east of the Entrance: tithe jars and scrolls in among the jars.

The text here is not easy to decipher, but if this reading is correct then we have in this item a clue to one of the most puzzling features of the Second Temple: the whereabouts of the Treasury. Josephus, perhaps advisedly, is very vague about the matter. He speaks of "treasury chambers" situated around the walls of the whole inner court (JW V v 2; §200) but elsewhere of a "treasury chamber" over which Agrippa hung the emperor's gift of a golden chain (JA XIX vi 1; §294). The New Testament implies quite definitely that the Treasury lay in the Women's Court, for Jesus sat down opposite it and saw the widow put in her two copper coins (Mark 12:41, etc.), and the incident of the woman caught in adultery took place "in the treasury" (John 8:2, 20).

Our scroll now seems to offer interesting confirmation of the New Testament topography since it places the Treasury "east of the Entrance," that is, in the Women's Court.

Josephus calls the area within the balustrade "the second enclosure," as we have seen. In this he uses a term missing even from the Mishnah, but found again in our scroll, in Item 40:

In the Second Enclosure, in the underground passage that faces east, buried at eight and a half cubits: 23½ talents.

127

In this item, as in the others quoted from this group of locations, reference is made to underground water installations. Unfortunately, the Survey officers were not allowed to penetrate the paving of the Haram to examine subterranean features which did not communicate with the surface and we are thus unable to confirm or deny the existence of cisterns in and around the Women's Court of the Jewish Temple. The cistern mapped by the Survey nearest to this location is probably still too far south to be identified with that of the scroll, but its description will give the reader some idea of the size and nature of these "tanks" under the Haram platform, many of which will be quite as old as the period of our scroll:

No. 5. In the south-east corner of the platform, has an entrance with a flight of steps at its east end, ascending southwards to the surface outside the platform, and a manhole at its west end, down from the platform. This tank is a long passage, with recesses on the north and another at its west end running south. The main passage has a semicircular vaulted roof, but the branch on the east is cut entirely in rock. The floor is 48 feet below the platform surface. The rock surface is 2,425 at the west end, and 2,408 at the entrance on the east, where are remains of a door. The former level is 10 feet below the platform level; the latter level is 8 feet below the present surface of the Sanctuary. The modern name of this tank appears to be *Bīr er-Rummāneh,* or "The Well of the Pomegranate" . . .[1]

Our ignorance of the subterranean features of this most important part of the Temple mount is the more vexing since it was the scene of one of those interest-

[1] Warren and Conder, *The Survey of Western Palestine, Jerusalem,* pp. 218 f.

ing anecdotes of the last exciting days of the battle for Jerusalem in A.D. 70, recorded for us by Josephus:

This Simon (bar Giora), during the siege of Jerusalem, had occupied the upper town; but when the Roman army entered within the walls and were sacking the whole city, he, accompanied by his most faithful friends, along with some stone-cutters, bringing the tools required for their craft and provisions sufficient for many days, let himself down with all his party into one of the secret passages. So far as the old excavation extended, they followed it; but when solid earth met them, they began mining, hoping to be able to proceed further, emerge in safety and so escape. But experience of the task proved this hope delusive; for the miners advanced slowly and with difficulty, and the provisions, though husbanded, were nearly exhausted. Thereupon, Simon, imagining that he could cheat the Romans by creating a scare, dressed himself in white tunics and buckling over them a purple mantle arose out of the ground at the very spot whereon the Temple formerly stood. The spectators were at first aghast and remained motionless; but afterwards they approached nearer and enquired who he was. This Simon declined to tell them, but bade them summon the general. Accordingly, they promptly ran to fetch him, and Terentius Rufus, who had been in command of the force, appeared. He, after hearing from Simon the whole truth, kept him in chains and informed Caesar of the manner of his capture. . . . His emergence from the ground led, moreover, to the discovery during those days of a large number of the other rebels in subterranean passages. On the return of Caesar to Caesarea-on-sea, Simon was brought to him in chains, and he ordered the prisoner to be kept for the triumph which he was preparing to celebrate in Rome (JW VII ii 2; §26–36).

Within the last few years extensive work has been done in and around the Dome of the Rock, even to the extent of removing some of the paving of the courtyard. To some extent the sanctity of the area has been "neutralized" by this work. Trucks have been driven up onto the Haram for the use of the workmen, visitors have been allowed within the Dome wearing normal outdoor shoes, and I was allowed on one occasion to take photographs of the Rock, previously expressly forbidden.

This, one might have thought, would have been a wonderful opportunity to press for permission to examine the underground area to the east of the Dome and perhaps lay bare for the first time some of its secrets. Of course, there would have to be no question of damaging the court and its paving, even though hair-raising rumors are current in Jerusalem that it is intended to rip up the old stones and replace them with solid concrete, in the same way as the beautifully weathered copper dome of the Mosque itself has been pulled off and replaced by a monstrous creation of anodized aluminum! It should, however, be possible to penetrate under the platform from an entrance made at one edge. We may reasonably presume that the upper platform is supported on vaulting through which one can crawl.

This, anyway, is what we proposed to do during our recent expedition. We found the local authorities most willing to assist, from the governor of the city to the custodian of the sanctuary. We had with us our surveyor who we hoped would be able to produce for the first time measurements and an accurate record of underground installations that had been covered in by the paving and which might in turn lead down into more of the cisterns and secret passages that honeycomb the ground beneath.

Suddenly, when our preparations were well advanced, the good will we had been shown gave way to mumbled evasions and shamefaced looks. It became necessary, it seemed, to consult the army, and after much delay, the answer came that the officer commanding the Jerusalem area thought it militarily inopportune to make our survey. By then it was too late in the expedition's timetable to take the matter further, and we had to leave this priceless opportunity unexploited.

The real source of opposition to our plans we guessed, and subsequent events seemed to confirm our suspicions. An article appeared later in a learned journal published by the French Biblical School in Jerusalem openly rejoicing at the miscarriage of our plans. It had been written by the foremost protagonist for the legendary nature of the treasure inventory, the same archaeologist who had earlier deemed it inadvisable to entrust the Arab authorities with a translation of its contents.

The records of the Survey officers are full of instances of frustrated efforts and lost opportunities caused by the shortsightedness and chicanery of local authorities and even their supporters at home. In those days opposition came mainly from the Turkish rulers of Palestine and local religious interests, and from certain officers of the Palestine Exploration Fund in England who saw these scientifically conducted researches as bringing their own pet theories on the topography of Jerusalem crashing in ruins. Having undermined his own health and seen some of his colleagues die from disease caught in the sewers of Jerusalem, Captain Warren returned home to find that the full publication of his results was not contemplated since they did not accord with the preconceived ideas of members of the committee. In desperation he made a pathetic appeal:

. . . to the ladies of England, to the "better half" of the public, whether they are content to wait, but would not rather that what is known should be published in detail . . . so that the rising generation may obtain the benefit. . . . Will not the ladies who went down the shafts at Jerusalem help in this matter, and thus give to the world the results of the work for which I gave away my health to accomplish . . . ?*

One might have hoped that in these enlightened days of a century later, attitudes would have changed and a new spirit of glad collaboration replaced the mutual suspicion and intolerance that has too often prevailed in academic circles. It seems that human nature remains the same, however, and until new blood and enterprise is injected into Palestinian archaeology, many priceless opportunities will continue to be lost.

* Charles Warren, *Underground Jerusalem*, London: Richard Bentley & Son, 1876, p. 20.

CHAPTER SIXTEEN

One of the more important buildings flanking the northern side of the innermost Temple court was called, according to the Mishnah, the Chamber of the Fireplace, or Hearth. In its four corners were separate compartments, and around the sides of the main hall extended a low stone platform. The hall was used as the sleeping quarters of the duty watch of priests when they were not actually on guard. While the younger men stretched out on mattresses on the floor of the hall, their leader, the elder of the watch, had a special place reserved for his bed on the platform. At a certain place a marble slab was set into the stone. It could be lifted by means of a ring fixed to its upper surface, and on the other side, dangling into the cavity beneath, was a chain bearing the all-important keys of the Temple gates.

Our scroll nowhere speaks of a "Chamber of the Hearth" but does, I think, refer to this building, and in terms which throw an interesting light on its history. Item 7 reads:

In the cavity of the Old House of Tribute, in the Chain Platform: sixty-five bars of gold.

The "Chain" seems particularly relevant to the Chamber of the Hearth, and two previous items at least fit very well with the same general location, as we shall see. This being so, the question arises why

133

this chamber is called by our scroll the "Old House of Tribute."

Herod, in building his Temple, wanted to create a masterpiece which would put his own capital city of Jerusalem on equal terms with any pagan religious center in the Graeco-Roman world, but at the same time he had to beware of alienating the sympathies of the Jewish people in his project. He had thus to keep as far as possible within the bounds of historical precedent in matters of layout and siting of the Sanctuary and its ancillary buildings. Just how far he succeeded has never been entirely clear, not least for want of evidence concerning its immediate predecessor, the postexilic edifice of Zerubbabel. Nevertheless, our scroll reference to a former name like the "Old House of Tribute" implies that at least the relative positions of the surrounding chambers were preserved even though their functions may have changed in the new establishment.

Nehemiah mentions a chamber of the Temple which may well have been the Tribute House of his time (fifth century B.C.). Apparently, while he was away from Jerusalem, a certain Eliashib, who had been left in charge of the Temple's ancillary buildings, took the opportunity of subletting to a rascal called Tobiah the Ammonite "a large chamber where they had previously put the cereal offering, the frankincense, the vessels, and the tithes of grain, wine, and oil, which were given by commandment to the Levites, singers, and gatekeepers, and the contributions for the priests" (Neh. 13:4 f.). Tobiah had moved in with all his household, and the righteously indignant Nehemiah took steps on his return to bring his lease to an abrupt end: "And I was very angry, and I threw all the household furniture of Tobiah out of the chamber. Then I gave orders and they cleansed the chambers; and I brought back thither the vessels of the house of God, with the cereal offering and the frankincense" (Neh. 13:8 f.).

A further clue that Nehemiah's desecrated Tribute Chamber lay on the site of the Mishnah's Chamber of the Hearth may be found in the tradition that next to the Chamber of the Hearth was an entrance called the Gate of Offering (*Qorban,* cf. Mark 7:11), which was opposite the shambles where the sacrificial animals were slaughtered and flayed. Furthermore, the Mishnah tells us that one of the rooms within the Chamber of the Hearth was called the Chamber of Offering. All this seems to confirm the idea that this building on the north of the Inner Court had been erected on the site of the old Chamber of Offering or Tribute of the Zerubbabel Temple and could still, in the first century A.D., be referred to by its ancient name.

Of the separate compartments within the Chamber of the Hearth, that in the northwestern corner was the landing of a flight of stairs leading to an underground passage and complex of rooms. This landing and presumably the installations with which it communicated were considered to be in the unconsecrated area of the Chamber, division between consecrated and nonconsecrated being marked by a line of flagstones set edgewise into the paving of the hall inside. The stairs provided a convenient means of escape from the holy court for any priest whose ritual purity had, for any reason, become impaired. Should he suffer a nocturnal emission of semen, which would render him unclean for Temple service during the following day, he could go down the stairs and, finding his way by a light kept continually burning in the passageway, gain access to a privy and a bath in the so-called Chamber of Immersion. A fire was kept burning there at which he might dry and warm himself, after which he could return to his brethren for the remainder of the night. In the morning he was obliged to leave the Temple as soon as the gates were opened, and this he did by the same staircase and underground passage which apparently continued northward until it reached the northern exit, called the Tadi or Todi Gate.

This staircase may be that referred to in Item 5:

In the ascent of the escape staircase, in the left-hand side, three cubits up from the floor: forty talents of [sil]-ver.

The treasure was thus hidden about four and a half feet up the staircase from the bottom, level with, say, the sixth step. Under the staircase was apparently a store chamber for salt:

6. In the salt pit which is under the steps: 42 talents.

Salt was used extensively in the Temple compound not only in the preparation of sacrificial meat but also to scatter on the Altar ramp in icy weather.

It seems very probable that the site of these underground rooms and passageways beneath the Chamber of the Hearth has actually been found. Two large "tanks" were discovered to the north of the Dome of the Rock, lying roughly north and south but inclined toward one another at their northern ends. The westernmost (No. 3 on the plan, Figure 17) consisted of three chambers divided by piers. The northern end of the main passage had been walled up, probably at a date considerably later than the original construction. In the same way, the northern end of Tank No. 1 had been blocked, but was still some 130 feet long and

25 feet wide. It was estimated that if these tanks were projected northward, they would meet at a point on the northern limit of the old Herodian Temple area, the most probable location of the gate called Tadi. Unfortunately, the Survey officers were not allowed to explore beyond the blocking walls, but they reported that where the tunnels were reckoned to meet "the ground . . . has a hollow sound." It would seem, then, that Tank No. 3 preserves the location of the old Bathhouse of the Chamber of Immersion, and its projection northward would have been the way of escape to the northern gate.

Another of the buildings skirting the Inner Court was called the Parwah Chamber, a name which occurs in the plural at II Kings 23:11 as part of the pre-exilic Temple (commonly translated "precincts" cf. "Parbar" at I Chron. 26:18). The meaning and origin of this name have hitherto been uncertain, although reference is commonly made to the Persian *parwār* "open kiosk, summer house, treasury." This seems now to be confirmed by our Item 31:

In the recess which is adjacent to the cool room of the Summer House, buried at six cubits: six pitchers of silver.

The Mishnah tells us that on top of the Parwah Chamber were the necessary facilities for the high priest to bathe during the ritual of the Day of Atonement. The story of the king of Moab, Eglon, recounted with such gory detail in Judges 3, confirms what we should expect, that the "cool room" of an eastern building was on the roof and, furthermore, that toilet facilities of the more intimate kind were also to be found there (cf. the story of David and Bathsheba in II Sam. 11). Doubtless the "recess" of our text was something akin to the Moabite king's toilet arrangements.

CHAPTER SEVENTEEN

Before the portals of the Temple building itself
stood the great Altar (Figure 16). It was a massive
affair of some twenty-two (forty-five, according to the
Mishnah) feet square and rising fifteen feet from the
ground, access to the top being by ramp from the
south. On the top a fire burned continually, its embers
raked by special implements which were normally
kept "in the corner between the Ramp and the Altar,
on the western side of the Ramp" (that is, the side
nearest the Temple). Among other details preserved
in tradition is that in its southwest corner were two
holes, "like two narrow nostrils," through which the
blood that was ritually poured over the southern and
western bases used to run and "mingle in the water-
channel and flow out into the brook Kidron." At the
same corner, set in the pavement immediately beneath the Altar, was a slab of marble which could be
lifted by a ring in its upper side and gave access to a
"pit" (*shîth*), presumably part of the same drainage
system.

Today the great *Sakhra* Rock under the Muslim
mosque is usually pointed out as the site of the Altar
of the Jewish Temple. The visitor can go down steps
into a cave hollowed out directly beneath the Rock
and gaze up through a hole pierced through to the
surface. Recent repair work in the cave has brought
to light the remains of a drainage canal, but no evi-

dence at all that it ever connected with an outlet to the Kidron Valley.

The great Altar and its drainage system may be the reference of the last two items of our scroll:

60. In the Great Drain of the Basin: vessels of the House of the Basin, the whole having a weight of 71 talents, twenty minas.

61. In a pit adjoining on the north, in a hole opening northward, and buried at its mouth: a copy of this document, with an explanation and their measurements, and an inventory of each and every thing.

The phrase "the Great Drain" implies a water conduit of considerable importance and may well be the canal said to have been constructed to carry away blood from the Altar. This drain is specifically referred to in rabbinic tradition as requiring a special levy on the Temple revenue for its upkeep. The word I have rendered "Basin" (*bāzākh*) is used elsewhere specifically for the dish or basin in which the priests carried blood, entrails, and incense in ceremonies on or about the Altar. It is possible that this pseudonym was chosen by our scribe for its relevance to the Altar ritual, and if this identification be correct, it would appear that the Altar utensils were hidden simply by being pushed along the drainpipe under the Rock. The drain ran southward from below the Altar's southwestern corner so that our scroll's location of the pit to its north is true to fact.

In view of what I have said previously about the comparative freedom with which the visitor can, for the time being, approach the Rock, it may be of interest to complete this section of our study by quoting another passage of Charles Warren's book, *Underground Jerusalem.*

I was visiting inside the Dome of the Rock one day, when I observed that there was something peculiar about the northern portion of the rock. It was early; true Moslems were otherwise engaged; and seizing my opportunity when quite unobserved, I vaulted over the high railing which encloses this morsel of Paradise and examined it. The rock presents a large surface, but I directed my attention particularly to one point, where I found two pieces of flagging lying north and south, in the continuation of a known cutting in the surface; at one place I could just get my hand in between, and found that there was a hollow.

With all the wonderful traditions about this rock, this was not a chance to be lost; for though I could not get into the Well of Souls from the cave inside, might I not do far better here? I had been told of a curious opening somewhere on the surface of this rock, where sixty years ago a man let down a plumbline, and all the string in Jerusalem would not enable him to sound the bottom. I had to be very secret, the risk was great, and not even the mosque guardians knew what I was about to do. For all these people are like children; if they think over the prospect of anything dangerous they get frightened and slink out of it,—dying a thousand deaths in fearing one. I always took them on the spur of the moment, and then when all was over, and no harm came of it, they forgot about their terror.

Accordingly, I made arrangements for visiting the great dome in the morning a few days after, and carried with me, concealed in my sleeve, a small iron lever, just the length of my arm; on calling at the Serai, I found, as usual, two Government zaptīs ready to watch over my actions, but I was equal to the emergency, for I was accompanied by three ladies who had courageously assented to assist in the undertaking. They were to distract the attention of the zaptīs and other officials while I was working away at the stone. My other accomplice was the late Capt. E. Warry, R.A., who was to look out and give warning and assist the ladies should any evil befall me.

At the gate of Mahomet was Corporal Ellis, ready with a rope and ladder as a blind, and Sergeant Birtles was to be late at another gate so that one of the zaptīs had to go back for him, and he was to look for me all about, and, not finding me, to wander round with the zaptī, but still near to the dome, in case we wanted to collect our forces. The other zaptī I sent to admit Corporal Ellis, and he, having his instructions, kept him waiting; and of course the zaptī, knowing that the rope and ladder were with him, thought I could do nothing harmful under the dome, and supposed I was waiting for him.

The Mosque officials and hangers-on then showed the ladies down into the cave under the rock on which I was to work: and I, watching the last man in, again vaulted over the railing, scrambled up to the piece of flagging, and put in the lever to prise it up. All this time my Moslem friend of the Mosque, who let me do the work and yet forbad it, crept behind a pillar, eyeing all the doors, in an agony of terror, ready to rush out, should I be discovered and swear I was committing sacrilege. I tried my lever on the most northerly piece of flagging, three feet by two feet six inches, and three to four inches thick; it was embedded in the rock with mortar, and as each piece crumbled off I carefully stuffed it down the hole I had made, so that should I have hastily to decamp there would be no sign of my having been there.

After about three minutes the flagging began to loosen, and I was able to get my fingers under it; but it was of too great a weight for one man, though I have powerful muscles for such purposes, and when I had raised the stone up halfway across the hole, I gave my shoulder a wrench, and my left arm hung powerless by my side. I had accidently injured again some muscles in my left arm which had been lacerated by a fall down a scarp which I had met with at Gibraltar some four years before. I was quite unable with my right arm to keep up the stone, and it fell with a crash into the hole below (which, proved to be only three feet deep), causing an echo which shook the building and reverberated all over the place.

All this time the ladies were asking innumerable questions as to the sights within the cave: whether the "tongue of the rock" could be persuaded to speak; whether Mahomet had his turban on when he pushed his head up through the roof; why Elias, David and Abraham should all have chosen praying-places so close together; and whether any voices could be heard in the "Well of Souls." Over and over again they insisted on the tales being told, and probably the showmen had never before found a party so bent on learning Moslem lore. When at last they heard the crash above them, and the echo around, they showed no signs of emotion though it was impossible for them to imagine what had happened; one, with woman's wit, silenced the arising suspicion of their guide by asking if the wind had not risen, as the door had slammed with a noise.

All this time my Moslem friend was in agonies of terror, and conjured me to make haste: and at last, when I let go the stone, he became frantic, declared that we should all get murdered, and that I must go at once; but I was on the rock, and he was not; and, as he could not even touch it with his feet (when I was near), I was on vantage ground, and told him to send in a man to help me get up the stone again; but he said, with a grim smile, how could that be, for even the Pasha was only allowed once a year to approach the stone? and added that if it was left it could be put back again in the night. I asked him whether he would get the Pasha to come and do it for him, upon which he tore his hair, and begged me to come away: however, I had now to make my observations, having run the risk, and dived down below into the hole.

I found that these pieces of flagging conceal a cutting in the rock about two feet wide and eleven feet long, running north, and in that direction blocked up with rough masonry. It was only three feet deep at the time, but the bottom is soft earth or dust, and I had no means of ascertaining the real depth. It is not easy to determine the object of this passage.

Sir John Maundeville, A.D. 1322, relates of this place: "And in the middle of the Temple are many high stages, fourteen steps high, with good pillars all about, and this place the Jews call the Holy of Holies. No man except the prelate of the Saracens, who makes their sacrifice, is allowed to come in there. And the people stand all about in divers stages, according to their dignity or rank, so that they may all see the sacrifice."

The Moslems, however, do not appear to have sacrificed here to such a great extent as to have needed a gutter for the purpose of carrying off the blood: indeed, some assert that the Moslems do not sacrifice at all; but that is an error. All the Arabian Moslems sacrifice at irregular intervals; it is one of the remnants of their original religion still clinging to them.

The solution I propose is that above this rock was the chamber of the washers of the Temple: here were the inwards, etc., cleaned, and this gutter carried the blood and refuse down to mingle with that from the altar, and then to run into the Kidron by the passage we discovered under the Single Gate.

But all this time the ladies are waiting down in the cave, and my Moslem friend insisting on my departure. Having taken my measurements, left the rock, and got on to the outside pavement, my friend was himself again. I wanted to go on again to try to put the stone in its place, when he became as frantic as ever. Asking his reasons, he replied, "If you are found on the rock there is only one thing that can happen; but if only the stone is found displaced, who can suppose that you have done it? It is Allah who has thrown it down." And said I, "Will Allah get it up again to-night?" to which he replied that he was sure he would. There was nothing more to do here, for we could not clear out the gutter in the daytime, and at night two black men kept guard, ever on the look-out for me: whether they helped to get the stone back again I cannot say, but a few days after I found that it had been got up again, and put in its place.[1]

This story is characteristic of the many such anecdotes in Warren's book and vividly illustrates the kind of antics that the serious investigator was obliged to perform to make his researches a century ago in Jerusalem. It is, at the same time, a reminder that even the present, more liberal attitude of the authorities can avail nothing if it is not matched in archaeological circles by the spirit of enterprise and opportunism displayed by men of Warren's caliber.

[1] Warren, *Underground Jerusalem*, pp. 402–7.

CHAPTER EIGHTEEN

Whoever buried the treasure of our scroll had access to the Temple before its destruction in the late summer of A.D. 70. This follows both from the nature of the objects concealed and from their hiding places, most of which lay in or about the Temple itself. As far as these deposits are concerned, any priest with access to the treasuries could have been responsible for hiding the treasure and for the composition of at least that part of the scroll. But what of the deposits about Qumran and the Dead Sea, and who laid the scroll in the cave?

It is possible that the Qumran Essenes had past acquaintances among the Jerusalem priesthood to whom, in this hour of danger, they were willing to lend their local knowledge of the Judaean desert for the concealment of sacred treasures and the scroll. Yet such a contact between Qumran and the city, in view of what we know about the Essenes and the strictness of their self-imposed exile, is difficult to envisage. Furthermore, the display of such trust by the Jerusalem priesthood to this fanatical, fringe sect, to the point of entrusting them with Temple secrets, seems hardly credible. It is much simpler to suppose that the concealers of the treasure in Jerusalem and about the Dead Sea and Jericho were of one and the same group, and that the Qumran Essenes had nothing at all to do with it.

A glance at a map of the scroll locations (Figure 18) will show that Qumran, Khirbet Mird, Jericho, and Docus form a clear line of defense on Jerusalem's eastern flank. The one group of Jews likely to have exercised control over these strategic positions during the war with the Romans were the Zealots, centered on Jerusalem.

The body of Jewish patriots owed their name (Greek *Zēlōtai*) to the overwhelming zeal with which they sought to execute God's will on earth, and, like other religious fanatics before and after, they were not averse to shedding blood in His name. During the first Jewish Revolt (A.D. 66–70), the Zealots played a vital part in whipping up popular enthusiasm for the war against their pagan overlords and were themselves quite as ready to die for the cause as to massacre any of their own countrymen who opposed them. If their name has become synonymous with cold-blooded murder and lust for power and their essentially religious aims often overlooked, this is due in a large measure to their first-century chronicler, Josephus.

No one will deny that we owe the Jewish historian a tremendous debt of gratitude; without his histories we should know very little about Jewish history of the intertestamental period and particularly of the conduct of the first Jewish Revolt. There is a growing awareness among scholars, however, that though he may have been a superb observer of military affairs and local topography, he is far less reliable in his reporting of matters of opinion, particularly where it did not correspond to his own. He was a thoroughgoing aristocrat, with little regard for the viewpoints of those less well bred and educated than himself. His distrust and bias is nowhere more marked than in his treatment of the Zealots and their cause. This is no doubt due at least in part to the fact that more than once he was offered violence at their hands and barely escaped with his life.

For Josephus and his class it soon became clear that the Revolt was almost bound to end in disaster; everything they loved best in patrician Jerusalem must be destroyed. Although he began the war as a Jewish Army commander in Galilee, where he first fell foul of the Zealots, he ended the conflict on the Roman side, urging his countrymen to capitulate while there was yet time. We need not doubt that his hatred for the Zealots was fully reciprocated.

Despite Josephus' testimony, the Zealots were not merely brigands, using the war with Rome to further their own despicable interests. Doubtless in the first two years of the Revolt, when hopes still ran high and even Syria's Roman governor was thrown back ignominiously from the walls of Jerusalem, many of the country's lawless elements flocked to the Zealot banner, intent on lining their own pockets with any spoils that might be going. But the Zealots who fought to the bitter end in the besieged city were of a very different caliber. Their methods may have been harsh, often bitterly cruel, but their aims were essentially religious.

The origins of their movement go back two centuries to another religious revolt, then against the Greeks and under the banner of the Maccabees. From that shoot sprang also the Essenes. As time passed, and Rome brought the short-lived political freedom of the Jewish state to an end, pious Jews began pinning their hopes more and more on a direct intervention by God in the affairs of His people; nothing short of a cataclysm on a cosmic scale could hope to unseat the present hold of evil on the world. Where the Essenes and the Zealots parted company was on the means by which this divine intervention might be brought about. For the one, it could be only by prayer and watchfulness, reading the signs of the times from Holy Scriptures and world events and holding themselves ready to march with God's Messiahs when the time finally came. The Zealots, like Judas Iscariot, grew tired of waiting and hoped to force God's hand with armed revolt and the martyr's blood.

Perhaps the greatest of the Zealot leaders was John, of the town of Gischala, near Tyre in Upper Galilee. By the end of A.D. 67 this whole area had been reduced by the Roman legions, and the great pincer movement on the center of the revolt in Jerusalem had begun in earnest. John and a few friends escaped and made their way to the capital, intent on reorganizing the central direction of the war. He found, as he had suspected, that the priests of the Temple were, on the whole, ill-disposed toward the war. Whatever its outcome, short of the realization of the eschatological hopes of the fanatical fringe of Judaism, the prosperity, even the existence, of the Temple and its authority were in jeopardy. A hasty, face-saving treaty with the enemy was the only hope.

To the Zealots, this priestly hierarchy were traitors to God and His Law, more careful for the material prosperity of the Temple and its vast priestly retinue than the principles and faith they were supposed to uphold. This eschatological war, once begun, must continue until God should decide the issue by direct intervention, though Jerusalem and the Temple itself be first destroyed. Beyond the city lay the desert, ever the sanctuary of the refugee and rebel.

At the end of November, John and his followers reached Jerusalem and set about strengthening the city's resolve to resist the Roman legions (JW IV ii 5;

§115). This meant, in fact, the liquidation of all opposition within the priesthood and terrifying the city's artisans and shopkeepers into subservience. The Zealots showed no mercy, dispossessing and imprisoning regardless of rank, their only authority a burning religious fanaticism. For, after all, this was a holy war, a crusade against the powers of evil in this world, with its goal the establishment of God's Kingdom on earth; the end justified every means.

John's support came mainly from the street mobs, the half-starved rabble that were a feature of any eastern city. For them, there was nothing but life to lose, even if their religious aspirations did not match those of their new masters. There were others too, reared in the hopes of the re-establishment of the Davidic kingdom, who also lent their aid, sickened though they must often have been by Zealot methods. Before long, however, John found reinforcements from outside the city, as the Romans advanced steadily through the country, driving more and more fugitives before them. They, too, had lost all, and sought only a leader like John and a cause worth dying for.

The end of the purge among the aristocracy and priesthood saw the Zealots in control of the Temple. Then followed a significant event which shows the Zealots in a rather more pious light than that usually allowed them by their chronicler. Having deposed the ruling high priest, they proceeded to elect a new one by the ancient method of casting lots. This biblical practice of filling high religious office by seeking some fortuitous expression of divine will had of late given way to more direct methods: first by buying such lucrative positions from the hand of the ruling power and then by making the office hereditary. The one was as illegal as the other. The Essenes, within their hierarchy, followed the traditional practice enjoined by the Law, as did the Jewish Christians in their wake (Acts 1:26), and now John and the Zealots showed that they, too, had a higher regard for the Law than its official interpreters had shown over the previous two centuries.

The Zealots still had opposition to quell, however. The priests made a last desperate effort to regain control and civil war broke out afresh. John called for help from the Idumaeans, that virile people of the south from whose ranks came the Herod clan. From Hebron they swarmed to John's side with an immediate enthusiasm which gives some indication of the reputation the Zealot leader had already created for himself in southern Palestine. One suspects that John had laid claim to Messianic office, by no means the first Galilean to have done so. In any case, he was soon firmly re-established in Jerusalem and in control of the Temple and its treasuries. He could now prepare for the inevitable siege; any day the first flash of Roman armor on Mount Scopus to the north of the city might be expected. This spring of A.D. 68 must have been the time when the decision was taken to hide the Temple's treasures, the sacred vessels and tithes. Everything that must not be allowed to fall into Gentile hands, or that must be safeguarded from wrongful use by Jewish survivors of the coming holocaust, must be hidden now, while there was yet time.

In fact, unknown to John and his friends, Vespasian was at that moment arguing with his generals against making a direct assault just then on the center of the revolt. The commander believed, wisely as it turned out, that before the final blow was struck, every possible escape route had to be blocked. At all costs, John's withdrawal to the desert, where he could carry on guerrilla warfare for years while avoiding open battle, must be prevented. Sixty years later, in the second Jewish Revolt, it was the Romans' failure to appreciate this strategy that held down their armies in Palestine for three agonizing years.

John now alerted his outlying defense posts. To the southeast, on the western shore of the Dead Sea, lay the giant rock fortress of Masada. This had been in Zealot hands since the first year of the revolt (JW II xvii 2; §408), and its garrison had, since then, been living off the surrounding countryside. They now began more ambitious raids into the towns and villages farther afield. Josephus puts this down to their taking advantage of the Roman delay in attacking Jerusalem. This is partly true, but it is clear that these were not isolated raids, but part of a preconceived plan. After each individual attack, the smaller groups would link up with large companies and go on to attack the more important and so better defended settlements. It seems highly probable that such an over-all strategy was directed from the headquarters of the revolt in Jerusalem. Part of the plan would certainly have been the accumulation of provisions and money for the war. With the Roman noose growing ever tighter about the center of resistance, John would need to ensure that his outer defenses were well equipped to stem the enemy advance.

One detail Josephus gives in his account of these raids is of particular interest from our immediate point of view. He says that among the places raided were "holy places" (hiera). The common interpretation of this phrase as synagogues seems hardly relevant, for such places were not usually the repositories of large sums of money. It is more probable that Josephus was thinking of religious settlements of the Essene type at

Qumran, and it might well have been at this time that the monastery there fell into Zealot hands. We know that the Essenes must have had a considerable store of wealth, since for at least a century and a half each initiate into the community had been required to pool all his worldly possessions into a common fund, as the Christians were also doing (Acts 4:32 f.). The prize at Qumran was even greater; the site had originally been developed centuries before as a defense post, and it could be so used again. Even today, from the tower, the visitor can have uninterrupted views as far as the Jordan River in the north and to the headland of *Rās Feshkha* to the south (Figures 4, 18; *PDSS* Plates 95, 117).

It has long been suggested that the last defenders of the monastery were not the pacifist-minded Essenes but their more warlike compatriots, the Zealots, and our copper scroll now makes this a virtual certainty. The date of the monastery's destruction by the Romans has been well fixed archaeologically and historically at June, A.D. 68, when Vespasian's troops reached Jericho (JW IV viii 1; §450), so that the Zealot occupation probably lasted about three months. During that time they will have engraved and hidden the copper scroll, compiling it largely from reports sent in from Jerusalem and other garrisons.

If the Zealots, then, are responsible for the writing and deposit of the copper scroll, they must also have hidden the parchment documents which lay with it in the cave. This does not, of course, mean that these works came from a Zealot library, for there is nothing to distinguish them from Essene literature represented by the other Qumran scrolls. It does mean that these and probably other scroll caches were laid by Zealot hands, and this throws light on another of the scrolls' perplexing problems.

Examination of the scroll fragments from one particular cave has shown that these documents were torn apart and slashed with knives before being thrown into the chamber in which they were found (*PDSS* Plates 47, 48). The damage could have been done after they were deposited except that one piece of a sectarian scroll is reported to have on its back a roughly scribbled tally list of some kind, written in a Greek cursive script. Secular Greek of this nature appears nowhere else in the scrolls apart from the unexplained marginal code letters inscribed against certain items in the copper scroll. One suspects, therefore, that this use of Greek was the work of one group, certainly not to be identified with the owners of the sectarian scroll thus desecrated. It would suit the situation if, when the Zealots drove out the Essenes during their raid on the monastery in the spring of A.D. 68, they found there the torn and slashed remains of a considerable part of the Essene library, pieces of which they then proceeded to use as "scrap paper."

The marks of destruction have all the signs of urgency but not necessarily of vandalism and could have been the work of the Essenes themselves. It must be remembered that this was an esoteric society: all members were required on oath to keep the community's secrets, and a number of their scrolls have been found written in code. In the event of a sudden emergency, such as the descent of the Zealot bands upon the monastery would have constituted, the Essenes would have quite probably cut and torn their scrolls to prevent their being read by unauthorized persons. How well they succeeded only those of us who have spent years trying to put the pieces together again and read them can tell! Mercifully, the scrolls could not be burned, since this is forbidden for any document containing the divine name. If it be asked why the Zealots should have troubled to conceal such disfigured documents so carefully before they, in turn, left in the face of the enemy, the answer is probably to be found in the rabbinic injunction previously quoted (p. 47) that before a doomed city was destroyed all scrolls of Scripture must be hidden away. As we now know, quite a third of the works from Qumran are of the books of the Bible, and even in their torn state this must have been evident enough to the Zealots. We have already learned enough of them to appreciate that their piety would certainly have prevented their wantonly leaving books of the Law to be defiled by the Roman barbarians.

Again, if the emergency scroll deposits were the work of the Zealots, this might explain the very different treatment afforded the scrolls in the first cave to be discovered. Here the Arab goatherd found the documents wrapped in linen cloths and carefully laid in jars. This looks like the handiwork of their original owners, the Essenes, and Cave One may quite possibly have been a store rather than an emergency cache.

Josephus says that the Zealot raids were directed against "holy places," in the plural. There is no reason to suppose that the Qumran establishment was unique of its type, though it was probably the largest in that area. There may well be more awaiting discovery, and a thorough search of the whole Dead Sea area by every modern means of archaeological and aerial investigation is long overdue. On the other hand, perhaps the sites of at least some of such "holy places" are well known already, for it has been suggested that the many Byzantine Christian monasteries scattered about the Judaean desert were built on earlier Jewish establishments of the Qumran type.

The pillage of money and food which Josephus makes the main purpose of these Zealot raids was not just wanton banditry. Money was required for fighting the Romans in what was clearly to the Zealots and their supporters a holy war. For this purpose, dedicated funds could be used, as the historian makes plain in the following passage:

John, when the plunder from the people failed him, had recourse to sacrilege, melting down many of the Temple offerings and many of the vessels required for public worship, bowls and salvers and tables; nor did he abstain from the vessels for pure wine sent by Augustus and his consort. For the Roman sovereigns ever honoured and added embellishment to the Temple, whereas this Jew now pulled down even the donations of foreigners, remarking to his companions that they should not scruple to employ divine things on the Divinity's behalf, and that those who fought for the Temple should be supported by it . . . (JW V xiii 6; §562 f.).

The melting down of sacred vessels is particularly interesting in view of our large deposits of gold bullion mentioned in the scroll, as for example in Item 7, where "sixty-five bars of gold" are recorded hidden in the "cavity of the Old House of Tribute, in the Chain Platform." John's belief that sacred materials could legally be used in the holy war is illustrated by another incident recorded by Josephus, where we are told that the rebel leader carved up some balks of timber sent especially from Lebanon for use within the Sanctuary. John used them to make some towers for his defense of the Temple enclosure (JW V i 5; §36 f.), despite the fact that they were dedicated material and thus banned for common use.

Similarly, money taken from "holy places" like Qumran would have been considered free for their sacred purpose by the Zealots, and it was doubtless this wealth which forms the bulk of the treasure deposited at strategic places around Jericho and the Dead Sea. Indeed, the valuables hidden under the walls and floors of the Qumran monastery as recorded by our scroll might quite well have come from pillaged Essene coffers.

Jericho was overrun by the Romans in June, A.D. 68, and with it Qumran and other Zealot garrisons in the area. Two years later, Vespasian's son, Titus, entered and destroyed Jerusalem. The Zealot leaders were killed or captured, but for another three years their followers held out at Masada. Only when that place had been invested and all its inhabitants driven to suicide in desperation could the Romans reckon the revolt in Palestine utterly suppressed.

The dust of war settled slowly over that unhappy land; the Zealots were dead or scattered into exile; their scroll of sacred treasures lay undisturbed and unclaimed in a cave by the Dead Sea.

CHAPTER NINETEEN

The copper scroll, then, is an inventory of sacred treasure hidden away by the Zealots most probably during the spring of A.D. 68. The treasure, which comprises dedicated produce and its containers as well as gold and silver in coin and bullion, comes mostly from the Jerusalem Temple, but may also include the fruits of raids made upon settlements in the Judaean desert, among them the Essene monastery of Qumran.

Undoubtedly the first need was to publish the text of the copper scroll, for the sooner scholars could begin work on resolving some of its still outstanding problems the more certain would be our future researches. As I have shown in Chapter Two, many of the readings proposed here can be regarded only as provisional pending further study and, if possible, the accumulation of fresh evidence. The difficulties in deciphering the text are great, partly through the problems inherent in reading a unique work written in an insufficiently voweled script and in a dialect not fully understood, but partly also through some special difficulties arising from the cryptic nature of the document, the idiosyncrasies of its scribe, and his apparent unfamiliarity with the square book hand he uses. Many of these problems will doubtless be resolved in time as scholars are able to devote themselves to their further study over the years. It is sufficient for the moment if my results, tentative though they must be, can carry the work another stage forward, into the realm of archaeological research.

It would, of course, be absurd to dismiss the whole scroll as fiction if, after two thousand years, the treasure no longer lay in its caches. On the other hand, unless it were removed soon after its deposit, there is some possibility that, in the desert locations at least, it is still there. Certainly there is no evidence that, prior to the archaeological investigations of recent years, the whole Qumran monastery, for example, was ever completely dug over, and even these modern excavations usually stopped at the lower floor levels. It can at least be said that one treasure trove survived in hiding under the floor of one of the rooms for the past two millennia (see above, p. 66).

A natural development of any properly organized excavations based on the copper scroll is a project called for from the very first days of the Scrolls story; the thorough investigation of the whole of the Judaean desert. Until recently it had been attempted only by the Bedouin, and a great deal of archaeological damage must already have been done in the course of this protracted amateur scroll hunting. The caves so ransacked must be considered sterile from the point of view of expert assessment of their occupational levels. Yet the fact that the cave in which the copper scroll was found (No. 3) and the innermost recesses of the last scroll cave to be found in 1956 (No. 11) were covered by falls of scree, and thus disguised, offers hope that the desert may yet secrete, in its wadies and cliffs, caves similarly undiscovered and pillaged. To find them, search parties will need to use every possible modern technique of archaeological science, including instruments for detecting hollows behind cliff faces and underground. Adequate means of transport will be required to traverse quickly large areas unsuitable for modern wheeled transport. The ubiquitous helicopter would be invaluable.

In the last year or two a start has been made on this major project. As yet we can work in only a limited way on very restricted funds. But at least a charitable foundation has been organized called the Dead Sea Scrolls Fund, that can invite public subscriptions, and already two expeditions have been mounted under its auspices (see *Search in the Desert* for an account of our first campaign in the Kidron Valley).

It cannot be expected that such a prolonged search as I have suggested will yield quick results. It will cost a very great deal in money and time.

At least we know now that the Judaean desert can preserve ancient manuscripts, and what, before 1947, would have been thought a fool's errand can now be considered a practicable and worth-while piece of research. If anyone in antiquity did drop a manuscript into a recess of a cave in this dry and desolate region, then there is a very good chance that it is still there today in a readable condition. This far, anyway, we have advanced from the pessimistic outlook of the experts who used to tell us that Palestine would never yield any really old manuscripts because the climate was too damp.

The great need, of course, is money, and in amounts that have never before been available to Palestinian archaeology. It is not even enough that there should be sufficient funds at hand for the immediate needs of the researches made necessary by our copper scroll. Undoubtedly the world is on the verge of even greater discoveries in this area, and just as the first finds of 1947 set off a train of further discoveries, so any major results yielded by these projected investigations could lead excitingly on to more, each needing instant exploitation. One of the difficulties of archaeological work in this desert area is that any hiatus between finding and full excavation can be disastrous, as there are no means for putting an adequate guard over the places located. A team finding an unworked cave with which they cannot instantly deal should be able to call up reinforcements while they themselves remain in the locality, hence the need for a helicopter and radio link.

The other great need is for a staff to man such great expeditions. Shortage of money for serious archaeological work in the Near East has hampered the training of students for many years now, and the fruits of this neglect are today all too obvious in the desperate shortage of archaeologists of top rank. It is also true, however, at least in England, that there has never been such popular interest in archaeology, stimulated largely by some excellent television productions. It needs only to harness such interest among the younger generation and to provide facilities and money for their training and later employment to overcome this shortage.

One would like to see one permanent result of Scrolls researches in the establishment in Jordan of an advanced institute for Near Eastern studies. To such a center could come men and women from all parts of the world to train and study with their Arab friends in all aspects of Near Eastern history and culture, entirely free from political and religious pressures. It would serve also as a pool of assistants for the kind of archaeological projects we have been discussing, immediately available and trained for any eventuality. Never again should the world let priceless documents rot in Bedouin camel bags while scholars stand impotently by, unable to move for lack of financial resources or initiative.

The Dead Sea Scrolls have the potentiality of a bridge between at least two of the world's great religions. They have come into the trusteeship of a third. Whether this potentiality can ever be fully realized depends on the ability of the world to keep their finding, publication, and interpretation free from the kind of obscurantism and sectarian interests they have the power to surmount. Perhaps in the founding and support of such an institution as I have suggested can be realized the means of fulfilling this bridge between the tragically divided factions of mankind; perhaps here, in mutual tolerance and understanding, the copper scroll may find its greatest treasure.

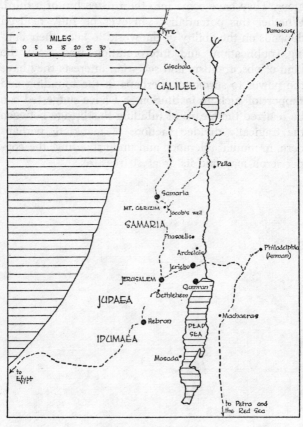

FIGURE 1. Palestine.

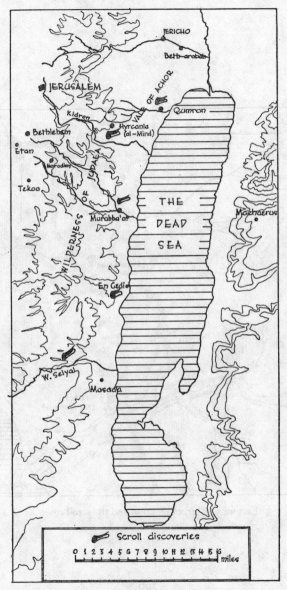

FIGURE 2. Scroll discoveries in the wilderness of Judaea.

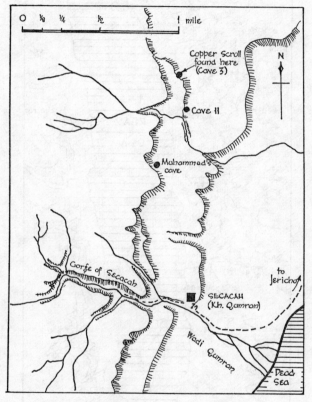

FIGURE 3. Khirbet Qumran and the scroll caves.

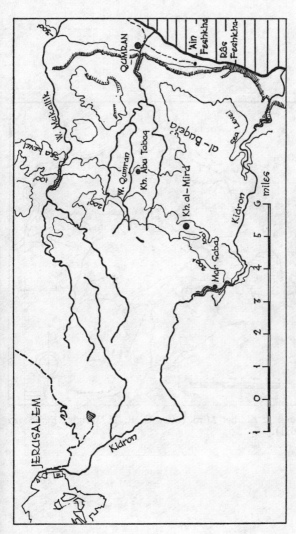

FIGURE 4. Qumran and the Buqei'a.

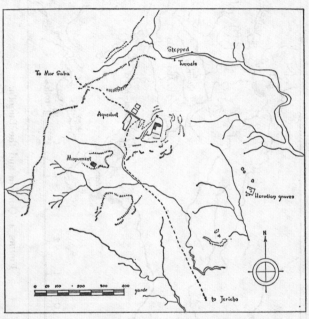

FIGURE 5. Khirbet Mird (after G. R. H. Wright, *Biblica* 42 [1961]).

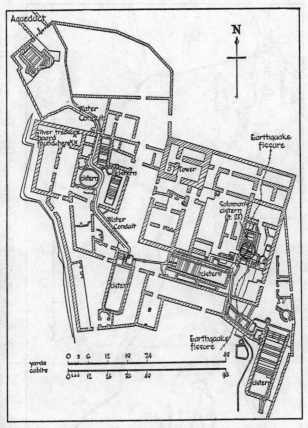

Labels within the figure:

Aqueduct

N

Water Conduit

Silver treasure hoard found here x

Earthquake fissure

cistern

cistern

Tower

Solomon's cistern (Jr. 23)

Water Conduit

cistern

cistern

Earthquake fissure

yards

cubits

cistern

0 3 6   12   18   24   48

0 246 12   24   36   48   96

FIGURE 6. Plan of the Essene monastery at Qumran (after R. de Vaux, *Revue Biblique* 63 [1956], opp. p. 576).

169

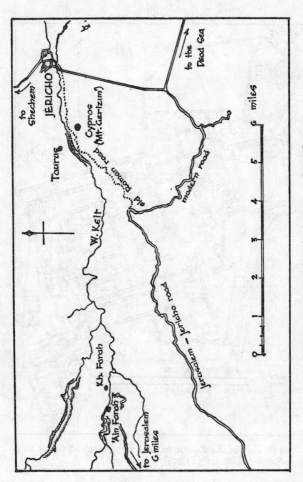

FIGURE 7. The Wadi Kelt, Cypros, and Jericho.

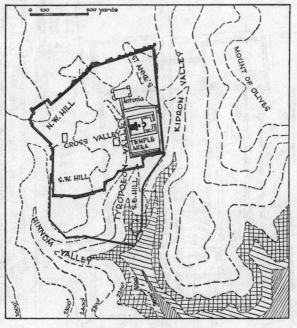

FIGURE 8. Jerusalem—relief.

171

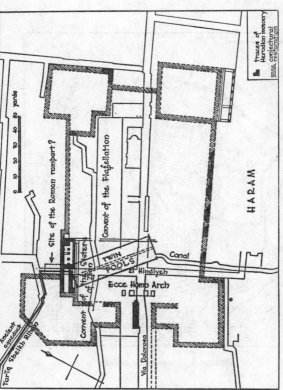

FIGURE 9. The Antonia fortress and the double cistern (after C. Warren and C. R. Conder, *The Survey of Western Palestine*, Jerusalem, London, 1884, opp. p. 234, and L.-H. Vincent, *Jérusalem de l'Ancien Testament*, Paris, 1956, pl. XLII).

Within the figure:

traces of Herodian masonry, conjectural restoration

Ancient aqueduct

Tarīq Sheikh Rihān

Convent of Abou Sisters of Zion

Site of the Roman rampart?

0 10 20 40 60 80 yards

Convent of the Flagellation

TWIN POOLS

el Hindiyeh

Ecce Homo Arch

Via Dolorosa

Canal

HARAM

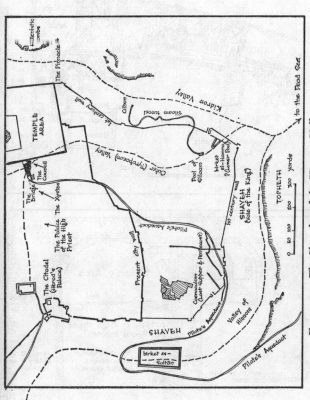

FIGURE 10. The Shaveh and the Hinnom Valley.

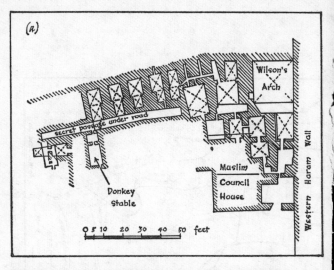

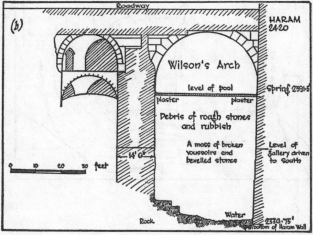

FIGURE 11 (a) and (b). Wilson's Arch, the subterranean vaults, and the "secret passage" (after J. Simons, *Jerusalem in the Old Testament*, Leiden, 1952, p. 368, and C. Wilson and C. Warren, *The Recovery of Jerusalem*, London, 1871, opp. p. 81).

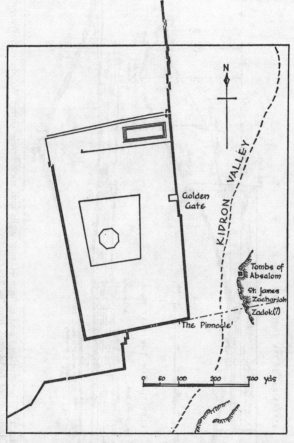

FIGURE 12. The Pinnacle of the Temple and the tombs in the Kidron Valley.

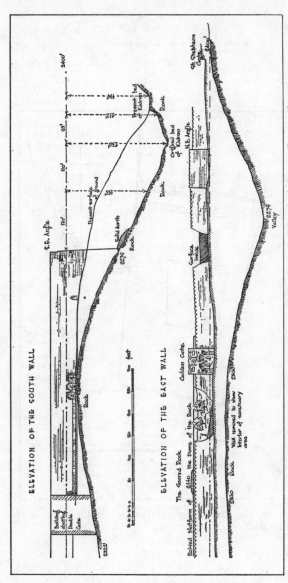

FIGURE 13. The southern and eastern Haram walls and rock levels (after Wilson and Warren, *The Recovery of Jerusalem*, opp. p. 119).

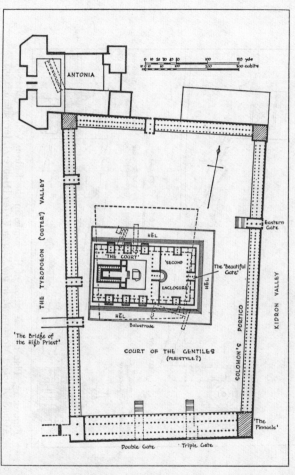

FIGURE 14. The Herodian Temple area (after Vincent, *Jérusalem de l'Ancien Testament*, pl. CII).

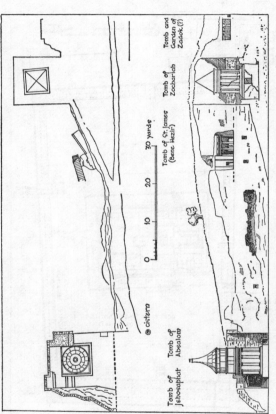

FIGURE 15. Plan and elevation of the tombs in the Kidron Valley (after N. Avigad, *Ancient Monuments in the Kidron Valley* [Hebrew], Jerusalem, 1954, opp. p. 38).

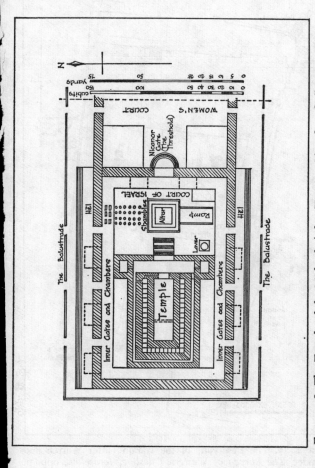

FIGURE 16. The Temple of the Mishnah (after Vincent, *Jérusalem de l'Ancien Testament*, Paris, 1956, pl. CV).

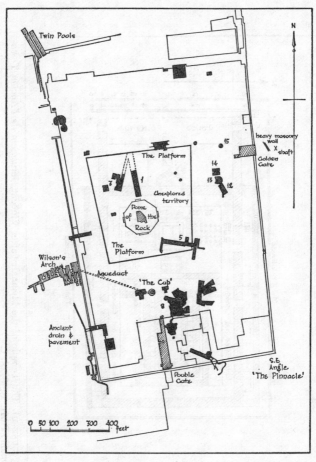

FIGURE 17. The Reservoirs of the Haram (after Warren and Conder, *The Survey of Western Palestine, Jerusalem,* opp. p. 116).

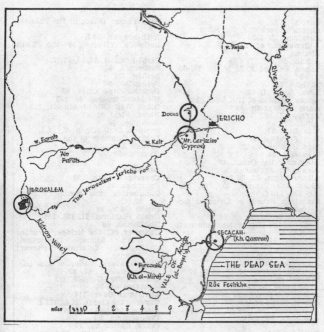

FIGURE 18. The treasure locations of the copper scroll.

SUBJECT INDEX

Aaron, 40 f.
Abram (Abraham), 98, 143
Absalom, 13, 105
  Monument of, 19, 25
Abubus, 75
Achan, 50
Achor, Vale of, 21 f., 50, 52, 57, 60, 64, 66
Actium, 65
Acts, Book of, 125
Agony, Garden of the, 108 f., 112
Agrippa, Marcus, 53
Agrippa II, 92, 127
Ahaz, 97
'Ain Dŭk, 77
'Ain Feshkha, 61
'Ain Gharabah, 63
'Ain Jidi, 63
Alexander the Great, 17
Alexander Jannaeus, 73
Alexandrium, 52, 73 f.
Altar, the Temple, 40, 117, 125, 136, 139 f.
American School of Oriental Research, 3
Amman, 29, 31, 33, 69, 76
Ananias, the High Priest, house of, 92
Anthony, 84
Antigonus, 53
Antiochus Epiphanes, 43
Antipater, 53
Antonia, fortress of, 57, 84 f., 87
'Aqabet el-Hindiyeh, 86
Aristobulos, 52 f.
Ark of the Covenant, 39 f.
Arnon, gorge of the, 73
Atonement, the Day of, 113, 137
Augustus, 53, 157

Baghdad, 40
Baker, Dr. H. Wright, 6 f., 18, 20, 30 f.
Baruch, Apocalypse of, 40
Basin:
  the Great Drain of, 26 f., 140
  the House of the, 27, 140
Bathhouse of Black Marble (?), 26
Bathsheba, 137
BBC, 29
Belgium, 55
Bernice, 92
Beth Kerem (House of the Vineyard), 19, 25

Beth Tamar (Place of the Palms), 14
Beth-arabah, 63 f.
Bethesda (House of the Twin Pools), 26, 83 f.
Bethlehem, 47, 52, 59, 67, 73
Bethsaida, 83
Bethso, 101
Bethzatha, 83
Bezetha (New City), 83
Birtles, Corporal, 80, 142
Black Well (Bîr el-Aswad), 123
Blood, Field of, 97
Borsippa, 40
Bowden, Lord (Dr. B. V.), 5 f.
Bridge, Chamber of the, 96
British Army, 80
Buqei'a, 50

Caesar, 129
Caesarea-on-sea, 129
Caiaphas, 95
Candlestick, the seven-branched, 40, 42
Chain Gate, 93
Chain Platform, 21, 133, 157
Chaldeans, 98
Chamber of. See Bridge; Hearth; Hewn Stone; Immersion; Lepers; Offering; Parvar; Tribute
Cheesemakers, Valley of the (tōn turopoiōn), 82, 89
Christianity, Gentile, 115
  origins of, 34
Christmas Cave, 114
Cistern, the Great, 21 f., 122 f.
Citadel, the, 94
Coenaculum, 99
Coins, dating by, 17
Commandments, the Ten, 39
Contenson, Henri de, 2
Cooking pots, 68
Council Chamber, Jewish, 95 f.
Courts. See Inner; Israel; Outer; Peristyle; Wood Stores
Coutts, Burdett, 80
Crassus, 43
Cross Valley, 83
Crucifixion, the, 95, 109 f.
Crusaders, 76 f.
Cypros, 72 f., 77

Damascus Gate, 86

Daniel, 40
David, King, 90, 94, 103, 137, 143
  tomb of, 41
Day of Atonement, 113, 137
Dead Sea, 1, 4, 16, 40, 52 f., 57,
  63 f., 69, 73, 75, 77, 113 f., 147,
  153, 156, 158
Dead Sea Scrolls Fund, 161
Dead Sea Scrolls sect, 16
Dedication, Feast of, 104
Diodorus Siculus, 75
Director of Antiquities, Jordan, 4,
  33 f.
Dispersion, Jewish, 45
Docus (*Dōk*), 24, 73 f., 148
Dome of the Rock, 117, 129 f., 136,
  139 f.
Double Gate, 23, 119, 122

Earthquake, 64 f.
Eaten, Mr., 99
Ebal, Mount, 71 f.
Ecclesiasticus, 122
Edomites, 52
Eglon of Moab, 137
Egypt, 49, 115
Eleazar, Rabbi, 72
Elias, 143
Eliashib, 134
Elisha, fountain of, 72
Ellis, Corporal, 142
En-gedi, 63 f.
Enclosures, Temple, 25, 125 f., 127,
  133
Esplanade, the, 22
Essenes, 16, 29, 50, 61, 66, 147, 149,
  151, 153 f., 159
Etan, 47, 99
Euphrates, 41
Eusebius, 106
Exile, the Jewish, 117
Ezekiel, 118, 126

Far'ah, Wadi, 73
Feast of Dedication, 104
Feast of Tabernacles, 91
Fire Wadi, 113 f.
Fissure, earthquake, 23, 63 f., 68
France, 31
French School of Biblical Studies,
  2, 32, 131

Gabinius, 52
Gabriel, 55
Galilee, 149 f.
Garden of the Agony, 108 f., 112
Gate. *See* Chain; Damascus; Dou-
  ble; Golden; Jaffa; Nicanor;
  Offering; Qiphonos; Single; St.
  Stephen; Tadi; Triple
Gauls, 59
Gehenna, 97
Genesis, Book of, 98
Gerizim, Mount of, 26, 41, 51, 71 f.
Germans, 59
Gethsemane, 108 f.
Gilgal, 72
Golden Gate, 109, 119 f.
Golgotha, 110, 112

Great Wadi, the, 19, 25
Greek letters, 155

Hakeldama, 97
Hall of Congregation, 68
Hall of Justice, Muslim, 95
Haram (Muslim Sanctuary), 41,
  83, 93 f., 99, 105, 109, 117, 119 f.,
  122, 125, 128, 130, 134, 157
Harding, G. L., 4, 6, 20, 29, 33 f.
Hasmoneans, 51
Hearth, Chamber of the, 133, 135 f.
Hebrew, 12, 34
  scripts, 10 f.
Hebron, 152
Hegesippus, 106 f.
Hermon, Mount, 75, 77
Herod the Great, 42, 52 f., 57 f., 65,
  72 f., 83 f., 88, 104, 117, 134, 152
Herodium, 59, 73 f.
Hewn Stone, Chamber of, 96
Hezir, 106
High Priest:
  Bridge of, 23, 91 f.
  House of, 92
Hinnom Valley, 81, 97 f.
Hollows, The, 25
Holy of Holies, 39 f., 144
House of. *See* Basin; Rest; Sum-
  mer; Tribute; Vineyard
Hyrcania (*Khirbet el-Mird*), 51 f.,
  58, 60 f., 73, 148
Hyrcanus, John, 41, 51 f.

Idumaeans, 52 f., 60, 152
Immersion, Chamber of, 136 f.
Inner Court (Temple), 96, 117, 125,
  135, 137
Isaiah, 50, 89, 106
Ishmaelites, 44
Israel, Court of, 126

Jabr (*gabr*), 72
Jaffa Gate, 94
James, St., the Just, 105 f., 110
  the tomb of, 106, 108
Jehoshaphat, 105
Jemimah, 86
Jeremiah, 40 f., 97, 107
Jericho, 17, 50, 52 f., 59, 61, 63 f.,
  69 f., 72 f., 75, 77, 147 f., 154,
  158
Jerusalem, 2, 4, 10, 15, 17, 29, 31 f.,
  36, 46 f., 51, 53, 57, 60, 69, 71 f.,
  77, 79, 81, 113 f., 117, 130 f.,
  134, 141, 145, 147 f., 152 f., 158
  fall of, 40, 129
Jesus Christ, 16, 29, 71, 77, 85, 95,
  103 f., 109 f., 112, 114 f., 117,
  119, 127
Jewish literature, 38 f.
Jewish Revolt:
  the First, 17, 92, 148 f.
  the Second, 77, 114, 153
Job, 86
John the Baptist, 73
John of Gischala, 87, 92, 150 f.,
  157
John, son of Simon, the Maccabee,
  76

Jordan:
   the country, 6, 9, 20, 30 f., 33, 35 f., 162
   Government, 4, 34
   Museum, Amman, 33
   River, 52, 73, 76, 154
   Valley, 60
Joseph, 44
Joseph of Arimathea, 109 f.
Josephus, 41, 43 f., 59, 65, 73, 79, 85 f., 89 f., 92, 95 f., 101, 104 f., 107, 118, 125, 127, 129, 148 f., 153, 156 f.
Joshua, Book of, 63
Josiah, King, 41
Judah, 50 f., 63
Judas Iscariot, 97, 150
Judas, son of Simon, the Maccabee, 75 f.

Kastellion (Hyrcania), 54, 62
Kelt, Wadi, 72
KHLT, 21 f. (Items 4, 11)
Kidron, 24, 54, 81, 83, 103, 110, 113 f., 139, 140, 144, 161
King's Garden (Vale), 98
King's palace, 92
Kippā', Wadi, 23, 63 f.
Kozibah, 24
Kuhn, K. G., 15 f.

Law, the, 152, 156
Lebanon, 157
Lepers, Chamber of, 126
London, 20
Lots, casting of, 151
Louvain, 55

Maccabees, 52, 60, 149
   First Book of, 75
   Second Book of, 40, 43
Machaerus, 53, 73 f.
Machine, cutting, 6
Madeba, 72
Manasseh, 97
Manchester, 4, 20, 31
   College of Science and Technology, 5 f., 18 f., 30
   University, 4
Maneh, 44
Mar Saba, 54, 114 f.
Masada, 57, 73, 153, 158
Mattathias, 75 f.
Matthew, 97
Maundeville, Sir John, 144
Meals, sacred, 68 f.
Melchizedek, 98
Mercy Seat, 40
Mesopotamia, 40, 49
Messiah, 17, 41, 150
Messianic kingdom, 17
Middin, 63 f.
Milik, Father Joseph, 32 f., 35 f., 55, 68
Mird, Khirbet el-. See Hyrcania
Miriam's well, 41
Mishnah, 75, 118, 122, 125, 127, 133, 135, 137, 139
Moab, 52
Moabites, 115

Molech, 97
Monument, sepulchral, 21, 57 f.
Moses, 40 f.
Mount, the Temple, 91 f., 103, 119, 128
Muhammad (Mahomet), 13, 143

Nabateans, 75
Nablus, 71, 73
Nār, Wadi en-, 113 f.
Nazarites, 126
Nebo, Mount, 40, 73
Nebuchadnezzar, 39
Nehemiah, 84, 134
Nibshan, 63
Nicanor Gate, 126

Offering:
   Chamber of the, 135
   Gate of, 135
Olives, Mount of, 103, 106, 108 f., 119 f.
Onias, 122
Onias the Circle Maker, 90 f.
Ophel, 90
Outer Court, 122
Outer Valley, 24, 82, 89 f., 95 f., 98 f.

Palestine, 34, 45, 51 f., 75, 84, 114 f., 131, 152 f., 158, 161
Palestine Archaeological Museum, 2 f., 15, 33 f., 36
Palestine Exploration Fund, 80, 131
Palms, Place of, 14
Parthians, 53
Parwah (Parbah), 137
Paul, St., 96, 115
Pavement, The, 85
Peristyle, Court of the, 21, 122
Perowne, Stewart, 74
Peter, St., 96
Phoenician script, 10
Pinnacle of the Temple, 104, 106 f., 109
Platform, Temple, 88
Poland, 32
Pompey, 43, 51 f.
Pomegranate, Well of the, 128
Pontius Pilate, 41, 46, 85
Portico, the, 26, 104 f.
Potter's Field (Hakeldama), 97
Ptolemy, 75 f.

Qiphonos Gate, 92
Qorban, 135
Quarantana, 76
Queen, Tomb of the, 23
Qumran, 20, 34, 50, 62, 66, 68 f., 147 f., 154, 156, 158
   Khirbet, 16 f., 64
   Settlement, 17, 44, 61, 65 f., 70, 156, 158 f.
   Wadi, 17, 66, 70

Rās Feshkha, 154
Rechab, sons of, 107
Red Heifer, 120
Red Sea, 115
Rest, House of, 26

Robinson, Edward, 79
Roman Catholic Church, 32

Saba, St., 53, 55
Sacred vessels, 152
St. Anne's Church, 83 f.
St. Anne's Valley, 83
St. Stephen's Gate, 83
Sakhra, es-. See Dome of the Rock
Salem, king of, 98
Salome, 73
Salt, City of, 63
Salt Pit, 21, 136
Samaritans, 41, 51, 71
Sanctuary, the Muslim. *See* Haram
Sanhedrin, 95, 107
Sartaba, Mount (Alexandrium), 52, 73 f.
Scapegoat, 113 f.
Scopus, Mount, 152
Scrolls, Dead Sea, 2, 10, 12, 16, 29, 154 f., 163
Search in the Desert, 114, 161
Secacah, 23, 63 f., 69
Serpents' Pool, 101
Shaveh, 24, 98 f., 101
Shechem, 51, 71 f.
Sheep Gate, 84
Sheikh Rihān street, 86
Shekel, 44
Shushan, 40
Siloam, Pool of, 98
Simon bar Giora, 92, 129
Simon, the High Priest, 75 f., 122
Single Gate, 144
Sirach, 122
Slaughter, Valley of, 97
Smyth, M. Piazzi, 100
Sodom, king of, 98
Solomon, King, 39, 83, 104
"Solomon":
  aqueduct, 23, 63, 67
  Pools of, 67, 99
Sophronios, 61
Souls, Well of, 141
Stephen, St., 96
Stone-of-the-Strayers, 91
Stone, circle (?) upon the, 24, 89
Strouthion Pool, 85 f.
Sultan's Pool (*birket es-sultān*), 99, 101
Summer House, 24, 137
Syria, 53, 84, 149

Tabernacle, 40 f.
Tabernacles, Feast of the, 91
Tables:
  golden, 40
  shewbread, 42
Tadi (Todi) Gate, 136 f.
Talent, 42 f.
Taurus, 73 f.
Tax, poll, 45 f.
Tekoa, 99
Temple:
  the Jewish, 27, 39 f., 45 f., 57, 71, 79, 85, 87, 92, 117 f., 125, 127, 134 f., 139, 147, 150 f., 157, 159
  the Samaritan, 71

Temptation:
  Mount of, 77
  story of the, 107, 109
Terentius Rufus, 129
Thracians, 59
Threshold, the Great, 22, 126
Times, the London, 29, 36
Tithe, 21, 45 f., 63, 68, 134, 152
  vessels, 68, 104, 127
Titus, 92, 158
Tobiah the Ammonite, 134
Topheth, 97
Transjordan, 72
Treasure hoard, Qumran, 66, 69
Treasury, the Temple, 24, 43, 45, 127, 152
Tribute:
  Chamber of, 135
  Temple, 47
Triple Gate, 99
Twin Pools, House of (*Bethesda*), 26, 83 f.
Tyre, 66, 150
Tyropoeon Valley, 82, 89 f., 94 f., 98

United States of America, 3 f., 30 f.
Upper City, 94

Valley. *See* Cheesemakers'; Cross; Hinnom; Outer; St. Anne's; Secacah; Slaughter; Tyropoeon
Vauban, 74
Vaux, Father R. de, 32, 36
Veil of the Altar, 40
Vespasian, 17, 77, 152, 154, 158
Vineyard, House of the (Beth Kerem), 19, 25
Vision, Plain of, 98
Vocabulary, 12

Wadi. *See* Far'ah; Fire; Great; Kelt; *Kippā'*; Qumran
Warren, Captain (Sir) Charles, 80 f., 93 f., 99 f., 120 f., 131, 140, 145
Warry, Captain E., 141
Watchtower, 23, 63 f., 154
Weight of talent, 42 f.
Well. *See* Pomegranate; Souls
Wilson, Captain (Sir) Charles, 80 f., 92 f.
Wilson's Arch, 92 f., 95
Wisdom of Jesus, son of Sirach, 122
Wodehouse, P. G., 32
Wood Stores, Court of, 21, 126
Wright, G. R. H., 56 f.

Xystus, 92, 95

Zadok:
  Garden of, 26, 108 f.
  Tomb of, 26, 104 f., 107, 110 f.
Zealots, 148 f.
Zechariah, monument of, 105, 108, 111
Zedekiah, 40, 98
Zerubbabel, 83, 117, 134 f.
Zion:
  ancient, 83
  Convent of Sisters of, 85

BIBLICAL INDEX

Genesis (14:17), 98
  (37:28), 44
Exodus (30:13), 45
  (38:26), 45
Leviticus (16), 113
  (23:14), 46
  (27:32 f.), 46
Numbers (6:17, 18), 126
  (18), 46
  (18:12 f.), 46
  (19:2 f.), 120
Deuteronomy (11:29, 30), 72
  (14:22–27), 46
  (14:28 f.), 46
  (26:12), 46
Joshua (7:24–26), 50
  (15:7), 50
  (15:61–62), 63
Judges (3), 137
II Samuel (10:16), 13
  (11), 137
  (15:23), 103
  (18:9), 13
I Kings (6), 39
II Kings (23:6), 39, 103
  (23:10), 97
  (23:11), 137
  (25:4), 98
I Chronicles (26:18), 137
Nehemiah (3:1), 84
  (12:39), 84
  (13:4 f.), 134
  (13:8 f.), 135
  (32), 84
Job (42:14), 86
Isaiah (22:1, 5), 89
  (22:9, 10), 90
  (30:33), 97
  (65:10), 50
Jeremiah (7:32), 97
  (19:6, 11), 97
  (26:23), 103
  (39:4), 98
  (52:7), 98

Ezekiel (40:15), 127
  (47:1), 126
Hosea (2:15), 50
Matthew (4:5), 104
  (5:22), 97
  (17:24), 43, 45
  (18:23 f.), 43
  (23:23), 46
  (25:14 f.), 43
  (27:6), 46
  (27:37 f.), 110
Mark (7:11), 46, 135
  (12:41), 127
Luke (4:9), 104
  (11:42), 46
  (22:66), 95
John (4:5 f.), 71
  (5:2), 83
  (8:2, 20), 127
  (10:23 f.), 104
  (18:1), 109
  (19:13), 85
  (19:41), 109
Acts (1:18 f.), 97
  (1:26), 152
  (3:2), 119, 126
  (3:10), 126
  (3:11), 104
  (3:14), 112
  (4:5 f.), 96
  (4:32 f.), 154
  (5:12), 104
  (6:12), 96
  (7:52), 112
  (21:28), 125
  (22:14), 112
  (22:30), 96
Apocrypha:
  Ecclesiasticus (50:3), 122
  II Baruch (6:7–10), 41
  I Maccabees (16:11–16), 76
  II Maccabees (2:4–8), 40
    (3:6 f.), 45
    (5:21), 43